THE BEDOUIN

Shelagh Weir

Museum of Mankind
The Ethnography Department of the British Museum
World of Islam Festival 1976

The Bedouin

Aspects of the material culture of the bedouin of Jordan

World of Islam Festival 1976

Shelagh Weir
Assistant Keeper, Museum of Mankind

Museum of Mankind
The Department of Ethnography
of the British Museum
6 Burlington Gardens
London W1X 2EX

World of Islam Festival Publishing Company Ltd

First published 1976
ISBN 0 905035 08 9 paper
ISBN 0 905035 07 0 cased

Published and produced by the World of Islam Festival Publishing Company Ltd.

Designed by Colin Larkin
Edited by Liz Évora
Line drawings by John Thompson Associates
Set in 10/11pt Monophoto Plantin 110
Printed on 115 gsm Blade coated cartridge

Colour origination: Westerham Press
Filmset by Westerham Press and printed in England by Westerham Press Ltd., Westerham Kent

Front cover
Roasting coffee beans in an iron ladle (*miḥmāṣeh*), Abū Rabīyah bedouin, Negev desert.
Photo: Shelagh Weir 1967 (© British Museum)

Back cover
Detail from a woollen saddlebag (*khurj*) for a horse, Jordan.
L 144cm, W 58cm
1973 AS3 3 (British Museum)

Contents

Systems of transliteration from Arabic

أ	'	ض	*ḍ*
ب	*b*	ط	*ṭ*
ت	*t*	ظ	*ẓ*
ث	*th*	ع	'
ج	*j*	غ	*gh*
ح	*ḥ*	ف	*f*
خ	*kh*	ق	*q* or *g*
د	*d*	ك	*k*
ذ	*dh*	ل	*l*
ر	*r*	م	*m*
ز	*z*	ن	*n*
س	*s*	هـ	*h*
ش	*sh*	و	*w*
ص	*ṣ*	ي	*y*

ة *eh* or *ah*, or *et* or *at*

Short vowels *a* or *e*, *i*, and *o* or *u*
Long vowels *ā*, *ī* and *ō*

I have attempted to represent the bedouin terms as pronounced, although there is great variation even in south Jordan. *Qaf* when transliterated as *g* is pronounced as in *game*.

List of illustrations

Colour plates

Black and white plates

Line drawings

Foreword

This book has been prepared to accompany one section of an exhibition entitled 'Nomad and City' which opened at the Museum of Mankind during the World of Islam Festival, April–June 1976. In compiling the book I have had a threefold aim: to give a pictorial introduction to the bedouin and their way of life, to describe those aspects of bedouin material culture which I have had the opportunity to study in the field, and to provide an extensive bibliography of works written on all aspects of bedouin culture. I hope the book will thus be useful to a wide range of people.

Most of the bedouin objects exhibited in the 'Nomad' part of the exhibition, and most of the information provided in this book, were acquired in the course of field work undertaken specially for the exhibition. From late 1974 to late 1975 I made several visits to Jordan where approximately three months were spent in field research and collecting. These visits were financed almost entirely by the World of Islam Festival Trust to whom I wish to extend my sincere thanks. I also wish to thank the Government of Jordan for providing air tickets, and the Ministry of Tourism and Antiquities in Jordan for help with local transport. The British Museum kindly granted me special leave of absence to conduct the field work.

I would like to record my gratitude to the following people who have contributed to the academic side of this research with help, advice and criticism. I am indebted to Janet Milne who has compiled the bibliography in a very short space of time. Dr Clinton Bailey, Fidelity Lancaster, Gillian Lewando-Hundt and Professor Emanuel Marx kindly read the draft bibliography and suggested further entries. I have benefited greatly from discussions with, and information provided by, Dr Clinton Bailey, Fidelity and William Lancaster, and Gillian Lewando-Hundt. In Jordan I received great help from Widad Kawar, without whom I could not have gathered the information on jewellery. I would like to thank, on behalf of the Trustees of the British Museum, H.R.H. Sherif Nasser Bin Jamil for generously presenting two valuable items to the Museum (see Plates 6 and 43). Finally, I wish to thank my husband, Dr I. G. Dunn, for all his help in the field and in the preparation of the manuscript.

Shelagh Weir

Introduction

In Arabia, settled peoples living from agriculture and commerce, and nomadic peoples dependent on the herding of animals, have co-existed since ancient times. The dominant feature of this vast area is its lack of permanent water and its meagre rainfall. The only areas where the water resources have allowed cultivation sufficient to support relatively large settled populations are along the coasts in the south and south west of the peninsula, and to the north and north east along the Mediterranean littoral and the Euphrates. The rest of the area is a wilderness of stony steppe, sandy desert and mountains. There, the only water is found in widely separated oases where some cultivation – mainly of the date palm – is possible, and in scattered wells which tap water sources often deep underground. In these inhospitable regions the bedouin have subsisted for over two thousand years and evolved a distinctive culture many elements of which survive today.

The name applied to desert nomads in pre-Islamic times was *'arab* (singular), *a'rāb* (plural). It was the Greeks who first employed the term more widely to all the inhabitants of Arabia. The bedouin of today still refer to themselves as *a'rāb*. Our word 'bedouin' is derived from the term used today by the townspeople and villagers: *badawī* (singular), *badū* (plural), meaning 'desert dweller'.

Traditionally, bedouin rely on herding animals for their livelihood. Some bedouin groups are camel herders, others rely mainly on their herds of goats and sheep. Each group exploits a different type of terrain according to the physical needs and capacities of its animals. Goats and sheep need frequent watering and food so the herders of these animals predominate in the steppes adjacent to the settled fertile areas where pasture is more abundant and wells are frequent and reliable. Camel herders are able to occupy the inner deserts because of the ability of camels to utilize scanty vegetation and to survive long periods without food or water. The nomadic existence of the bedouin is dictated by their constant search for pasture and water for their animals.

Every bedouin inherits membership of a tribe through the male line. Tribes and confederations of tribes formerly inhabited and controlled their own territories. The smallest independent unit among the bedouin comprises a man and his wife, their unmarried children and perhaps an older relative, who all live in the same tent. Several tents of the same tribe, whose inhabitants are closely related by descent or marriage, often join together on a seasonal basis to exploit pasture and water in the same locality (Plate 1). Larger groups only form in response to particular political or economic conditions. Thus large numbers of tribesmen formerly gathered under a powerful leader at times of war, and many hundreds of tents from the same tribe congregated at large wells and oases in the summer.

Today many changes are taking place among the bedouin throughout Arabia. Products of twentieth century technology have been imported into their tent life. Some groups have settled in villages and taken up agriculture, attracted by educational and health facilities and in response to government pressures. Many bedouin work for oil companies or in government offices. However, while individuals take advantage of the opportunity to work in the cities, other members of their tribal group often persist in their life of nomadic pastoralism in the desert, reluctant to give up such a reliable and independent means of subsistence.

A major characteristic of traditional bedouin culture is the effective exploitation of their richest resource, their animals. They consume the milk and meat of camels, sheep and goats, they make utensils from their skins, they weave textiles and tent cloth from their wool and hair, they burn camel dung as fuel, they transport themselves and their belongings on the backs of camels, and they sell animals when they need money to buy those commodities which they cannot provide for themselves. The text which follows focuses on both categories of bedouin material possessions, those they make themselves and those they buy from itinerant merchants or in the markets of the towns and villages in the settled areas. An attempt is also made to indicate the significance of the various objects in the everyday life of the bedouin.

The information provided in this book was collected among various groups of the Ḥuwayṭāt tribe in south Jordan, and from craftsmen in the towns of Jordan and Syria who once made articles for sale to bedouin throughout the area. The Ḥuwayṭāt groups I visited are today primarily sheep and goat herders, though some have changed from camel herding only recently. Many Ḥuwayṭāt have given up their nomadic way of life during the last two decades and taken up agriculture. All the Arabic terms given are used by the Ḥuwayṭāt except those relating to objects from other tribes and areas and to silverworking techniques. For comparative purposes some written and pictorial material relating to bedouin outside Jordan has been included. In the space available it has not been possible to make comparisons with information on bedouin material culture published elsewhere, but other sources of information on the subject of each section have been cited.

The tent

The bedouin tent is ideally suited to the desert environment and the nomadic way of life. It is very simple in its construction and therefore easy to erect and dismantle. The cloth can be rolled up and, with the poles, loaded onto a camel for transportation. The tent cloth expands when wet and becomes waterproof in the rain. The interior of the tent is snug and warm in winter when a fire is lit inside. The tent walls can be arranged with a degree of flexibility according to circumstances. The front wall is usually removed during the day unless the weather is bad or privacy is required, and side and back walls can be hitched up to improve ventilation in the heat. Economically the tent is an extremely effective solution to the problem of shelter utilizing as it does the only available and plentiful raw material: the hair and wool of animals.

The tent is called *al-bayt* or *bayt al-sha'ar* ('house' or 'house of hair'). The main components of the tent are the roof, walls, poles and guy ropes. The roof is a rectangular cloth supported in the centre and at the edges on poles and anchored by guy ropes. The walls are pinned to the edge of the roof (Plate 4). The centre poles are about 2.2 metres high and the side poles about 1.5 metres. Tents vary in length – the longer the tent the more centre poles it has – but do not vary greatly in width.

The roof (*shgāg*) is made up of strips (*shuggah*) of goat hair cloth, each 60 to 80 cm wide, sewn together to run the length of the tent (Plate 2). Most roofs are made up of six or eight strips, half on each side of the central ridge. One or two strips are usually replaced each year as they become worn. The roof can hang down at each end to form side walls (*ruffah*). The roof is protected from wear by wooden sockets (*wāwīyeh*) or sticks (*gatab*) above the centre poles. There is no ridge pole. At the lines of greatest strain, narrow bands (*ṭarīgah*) about 12 cm wide are sewn to the roof from front to back. These run over the sockets and poles and have attached at each end wooden V-shaped stirrups (*'agafah*), often made from a forked branch (Fig. 3). Each guy rope (*ḥabl*) is looped through one of these, and the end secured by a simple knot which can easily be tightened or slackened. At each end of the tent short reinforcing bands are sewn along the top of the ridge to take the strain of the side guy ropes which are also attached to stirrups. The tops of the side, front and back poles, are hooked into the stirrups or fit into sockets like the centre poles. All the guys extend some distance from the tent and are secured in the ground with metal pegs (*watad*). The back wall (*ruwāg*) consists of two main strips of goat hair and wool cloth, usually with cotton stripes, and is

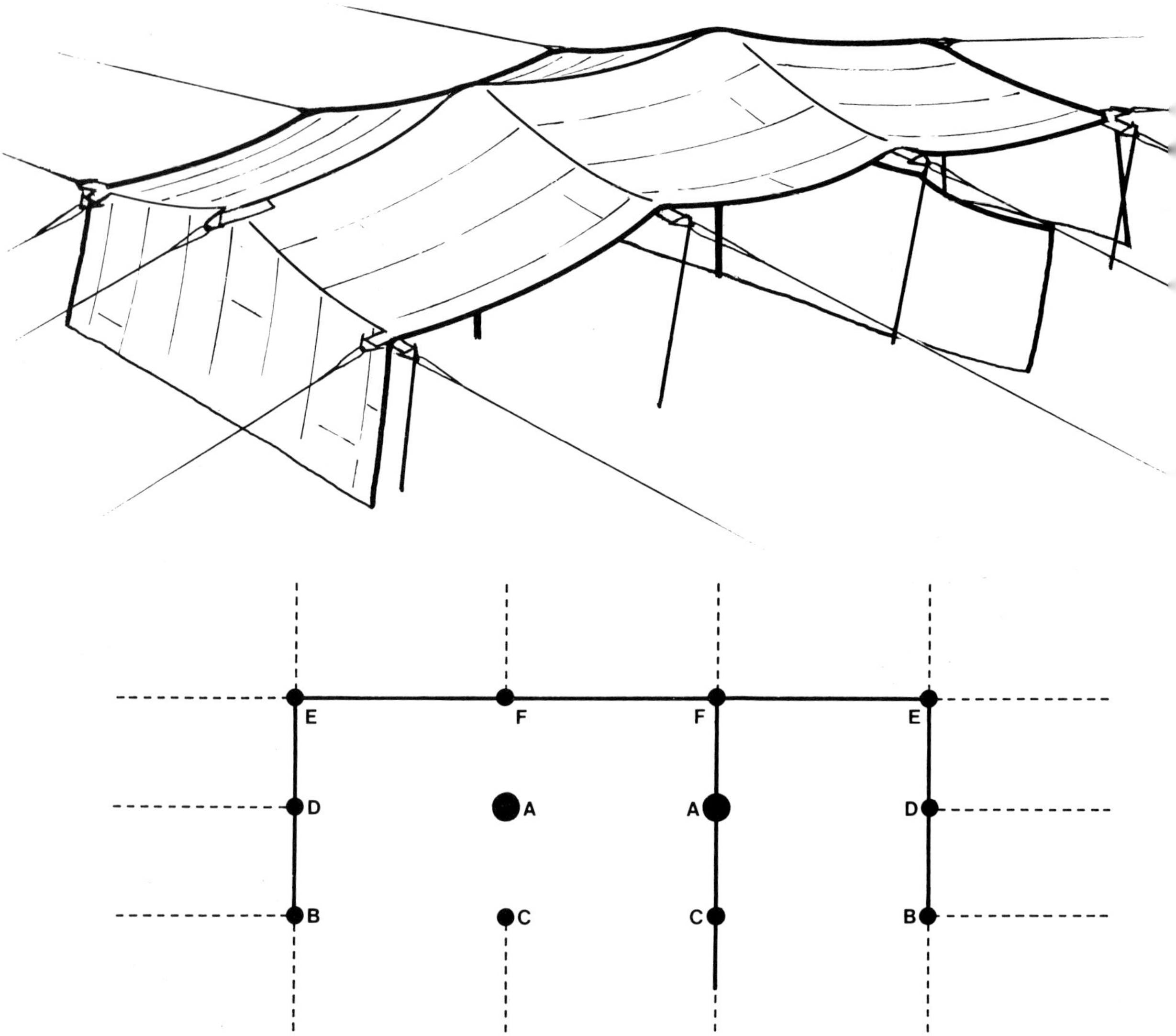

Fig. 1. The bedouin tent and plan view.

A	the centre poles	*wāsaṭ*
B	the front corner poles	*yid*
C	the front poles	*migdim*
D	the side poles	*'āmr*
E	the back corner poles	*rijil*
F	the back poles	*zāfireh* or *mākher*

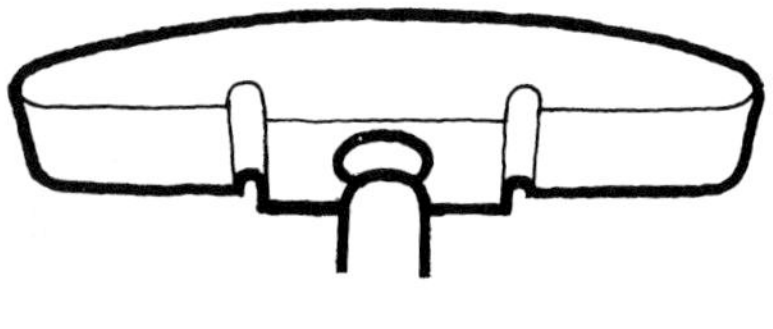

Fig. 2. Socket (*wāwīyeh*) for centre pole.

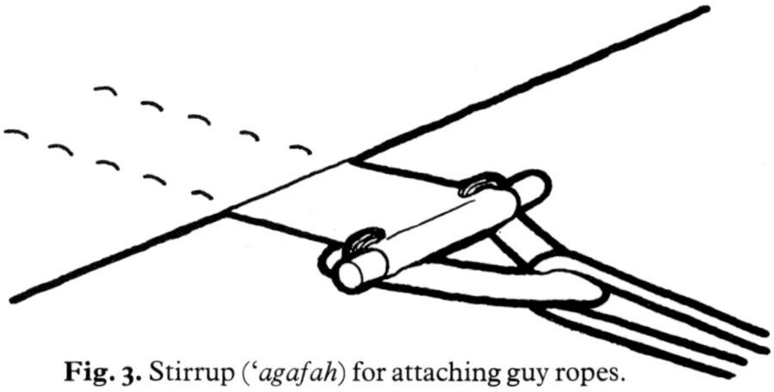

Fig. 3. Stirrup (*'agafah*) for attaching guy ropes.

attached to the roof with wooden pins (*khilāl*) pushed through vertically (Plate 4). When the roof does not hang to the ground at each end of the tent, the back wall is longer and is continued round to form side walls. The front wall (*stār*) is made from plain goat hair and wool cloth, and is attached to the roof in the same way as the back wall. Along the front and back edges of the roof and the top edge of the walls there is often a narrow strip of cloth (*makhal*) of inferior quality which can be removed and replaced cheaply when it becomes worn from repeated pinning. The walls also have a strip (*sfāleh*) of inferior cloth or sacking along the lower edge where there is the greatest wear from the rough ground. The tent is normally divided into two sections by a woven curtain (*sāḥah*) which is suspended from the tent poles.

Body imagery is used in some of the terms applied to parts of the tent. The front corner poles (*yid*) are called 'hands', and the back corner poles (*rijil*) 'legs'. The front of the tent is the 'face' (*wujh al-bayt*), and the back 'the back of the head' (*gafā al-bayt*). Other terms used are *bāhireh* for the space between the main poles and *shādaḥ* for the area under the back wall when it is stretched outwards from the tent by means of vertical bands (*ṭarīgah*) to make more space inside. Tents are differentiated by the number of centre poles (*wāsaṭ*) they have, and vary in size according to the size and wealth of the family. A one poled tent is called *gaṭbeh*, two poled, *fāzah* or *wāsaṭayn*, three poled, *mthowlath*, four poled, *mrūba'* and five poled, *mkhūmas*. Among the Ḥuwayṭāt in south Jordan today, the tents are mostly two or three poled. The space between the poles varies, but is usually between 3 and 4 metres, so a two poled tent is 9 to 12 metres long, and a three poled tent 12 to 16 metres long. The width of the tent is usually 3.5 to 4.5 metres.

Other sources of information on this subject include the following: Ashkenazi (1938: pp. 117–129), de Boucheman (1934: pp. 96–115), Dalman (1928–42), Dickson (1949: pp. 66–107), Dostal (1967), Feilberg (1944), Jaussen (1908: pp. 74–77), Musil (1928: pp. 61–85) and Peters (1952).

1. A Ḥuwayṭāt encampment in south Jordan. Photo: I. G. Dunn 1975.

2. Women sewing together the strips (*shgāg*) for the tent roof, Ḥilalāt bedouin, south Jordan.
Photo: Shelagh Weir 1974.

3. Erecting a tent, Ḥilalāt bedouin, south Jordan.
Photo: Shelagh Weir 1974.

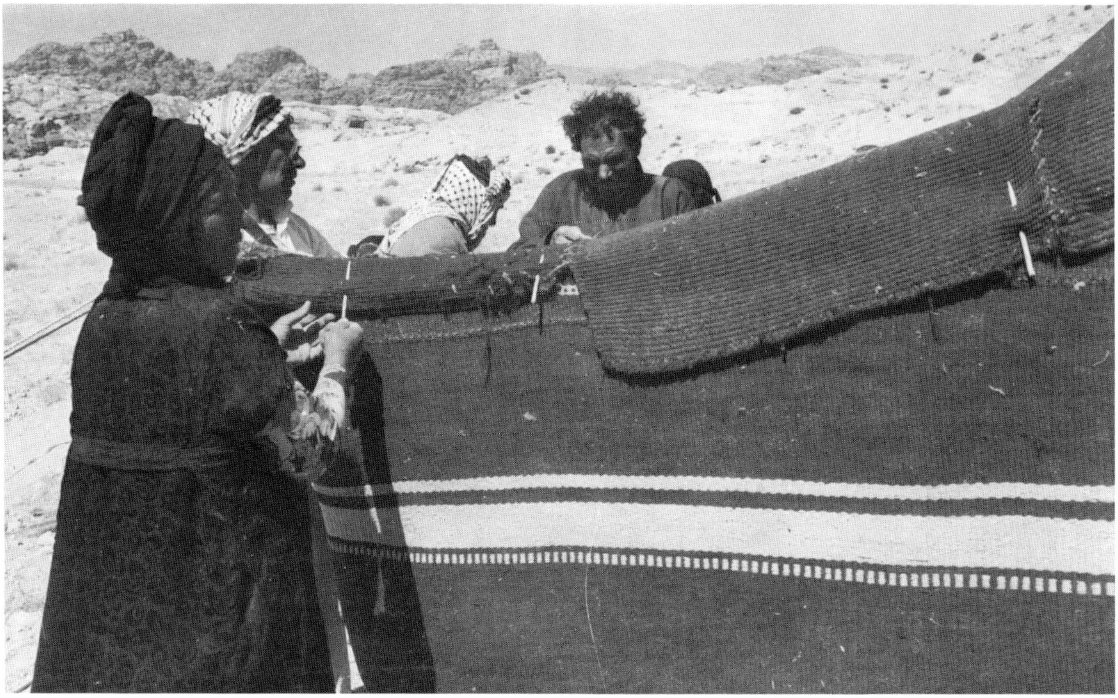

4. Pinning the back wall (*ruwāg*) to the roof of the tent. Ḥilalāt bedouin, south Jordan. Photo: Shelagh Weir 1974.

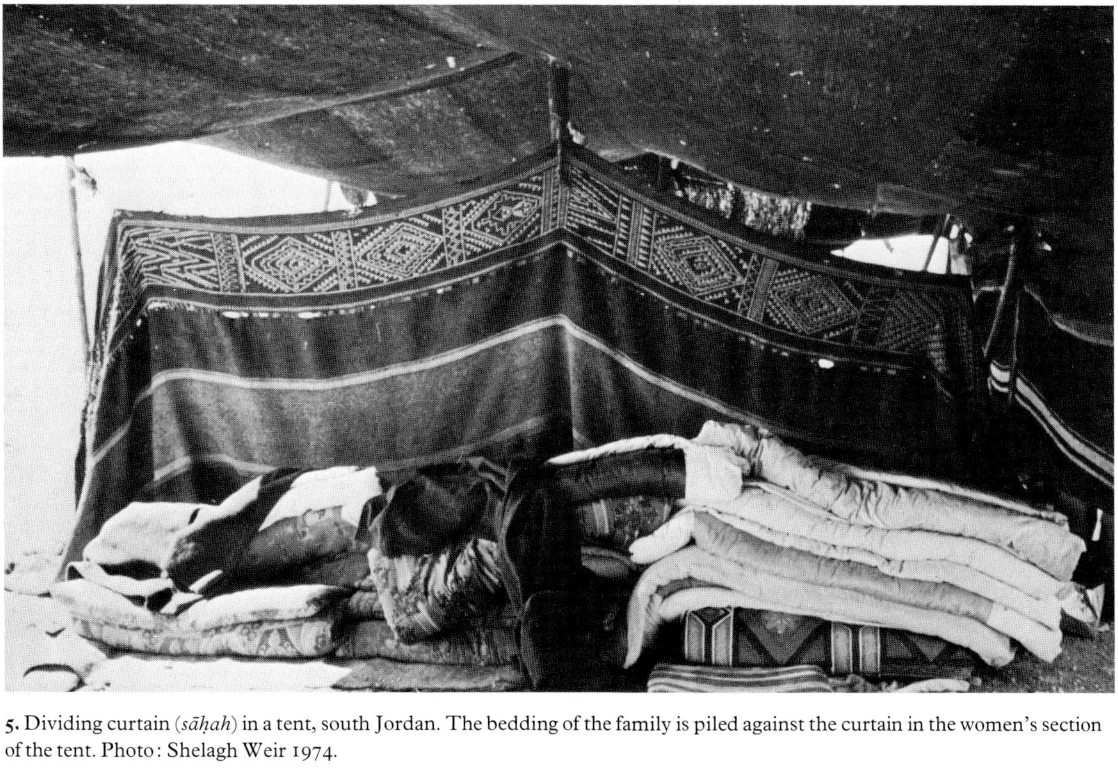

5. Dividing curtain (*sāḥah*) in a tent, south Jordan. The bedding of the family is piled against the curtain in the women's section of the tent. Photo: Shelagh Weir 1974.

6. Wall (*zirb*) of reeds decorated with orange, red, black and white wool. These walls are made by craftsmen in Syrian towns, and used by the Syrian bedouin and the Rwāla in north east Jordan to create a draught-free area around the fire in the women's section of the tent. They are made by winding the wool round each reed individually before joining the reeds together with diagonally and longitudinally twined woollen threads. This is a particularly fine piece which would be considered a luxurious addition to any tent.
Total L 7m, H 165cm (British Museum). Presented by H.R.H. Sherif Nasser Bin Jamil.

Domestic life

A man normally moves into a tent of his own when he gets married. He may start with a one poled tent, and enlarge it to a two poled tent as his family grows. The inhabitants of a tent are typically the nuclear family, plus perhaps an elderly female relative; a mother or aunt of the husband. A shaykh will normally have a larger tent than others, a three or four poled tent, as befits his status and his role as chief dispenser of hospitality on behalf of his tribal kin group or camping unit.

The social and physical needs of the inhabitants of a tent are met in the simplest manner and with the minimum of material possessions. One requirement, characteristic of most Muslim societies, is that the two main spheres of everyday life, the public and the private, should be separated. In a bedouin tent this is achieved by means of a curtain (*sāḥah*) which is suspended between the front and back of the tent so as to divide it into two compartments. One section is the men's domain where they receive visitors, entertain guests and meet to discuss tribal affairs. The other is the domain of women where they prepare food, take care of their children, entertain their friends and where the whole family sleeps. The tent dividing wall is always suspended from the tent poles, so one, two and three poled tents are divided either into one third/two third sections, or half and half. The relative size of the two sections of the tent depends on the size of the tent and the needs of the inhabitants. A shaykh's tent will have a bigger men's section than the tent of a large family, where the need to provide an adequate sleeping, storage and cooking area is a priority.

The men's section *(al-shigg)*

If the dividing curtain is patterned, as is often the case, the good side is always turned towards the men's section. When guests are present, the curtain is often extended out further along the guy rope to provide greater privacy for the women on the other side. Although women are supposed to keep out of sight when their husbands are entertaining, in practice they often peer over the dividing curtain and shout comments from their part of the tent. (Their seclusion has its advantages as it provides them with an opportunity men are denied, of overhearing men's discussions in the tents of other women they visit. Thus women often have greater knowledge of tribal affairs than one would suppose.)

The focal point of the men's section is the fireplace. Here the various utensils used for making tea and coffee are kept including coffee pots (*dilāl*, singular: *dalleh*), an enamel jug (*ibrīg*) for coffee grounds, a kettle for tea, glasses, coffee cups, tongs for tending the fire, and a tripod. There is usually little else in the men's section, except perhaps a camel saddle in one corner, until guests arrive. Then the rugs and mattresses are brought from the women's section where they are stored, and laid out on three sides of the men's section, and cushions are piled up at intervals for the guests to recline on.

7. Guests seated around the hearth in the tent of a prosperous shaykh of the Ibn Sha'alān (Rwāla) bedouin, north east Jordan. Photo: William Lancaster 1973.

The preparation of coffee

The fireplace is normally situated at the front of the tent in the centre of the men's section, and is a shallow rectangular depression with a mound at its front edge formed by the scooped out earth. The tea and coffee are usually prepared by the host himself. Upon the arrival of a visitor, tea is brewed up in a kettle and poured into a small glass with sugar, then, if coffee is not already simmering in a pot on the fire, fresh coffee will be made. The utensils used for making coffee are illustrated in Plates 10–14. Dried camel dung and small bushes, such as the fragrant wormwood (*shīḥ*), which grow all over south Jordan, are used for fuel. The beans are taken from their con-

8. Serving coffee in a tent of the Ibn Jāzi bedouin, south Jordan. The coffee is always poured with the left hand into a small cup, with no handle, held in the right. On the right is a brass coffee mortar. Photo: I. G. Dunn 1975.

tainer, traditionally a decorated skin bag (*mijrabat al-gahweh*) hanging from a centre pole, and placed in an iron ladle (*miḥmāṣeh*) over the fire. As the beans roast they are stirred with a rod (*yad*) to prevent them burning (cover). They are then turned out into a wooden cooling dish (*mabradah*) which is usually oval or rectangular in shape. (The dish in the form of an animal illustrated in Plate 11 is very unusual.) When the beans have cooled they are poured from the dish, which usually has a spout for this purpose, into a mortar. In south Jordan wooden mortars (*mihbāsh* or *nijir*) carved with geometric designs are the most common, although brass mortars (*miḥwān*) are also used (Plate 8). The host pounds the beans with the pestle (*yad*) in a rhythmic beat which can be heard for some distance and advertizes the presence of guests to the rest of the encampment. Meanwhile the largest of three or four coffee pots has been filled with water and placed on the fire. When the water boils, the ground coffee is tossed in, and the pot is returned to the fire and allowed to rise to the boil several times. Then a few cardamom seeds (*hayl*) are pounded in the mortar and put in another smaller pot, and the coffee is poured over them and allowed to simmer. It is then strained into a third smaller pot from which it is poured into the cups. Some coffee pots have a lid on the spout, or sticks are stuffed down it, to prevent the grounds and seeds escaping. Coffee is always poured with the pot in the left hand and the cup or cups in the right (Plate 8). The cups (*finjān* or *finjāl*) used by the bedouin are very small and have no handles. Only a little coffee is poured into each cup, and each guest is offered three helpings after which it is polite to indicate that one has had sufficient by shaking the cup when handing it back to the host.

The bedouin are famous for their hospitality, and it is impossible to visit even the poorest tent without being offered tea or coffee with the greatest grace and dignity. The ceremony of making coffee is not merely a way of extending friendliness and giving refreshment to a weary traveller, but is in a deeper sense a physical statement of the obligation a host incurs in welcoming a visitor into his home. Henceforth he is bound by a strict code of honour to offer protection to his guest whoever he may be.

Often a host will also insist on providing food for his visitor, and will call to his wife to prepare bread and eggs. The ultimate expression of hospitality is to slaughter a sheep or goat. Meat is a luxury, and animals are normally only slaughtered on special occasions such as when there are important guests (Plate 16), or for the celebration of a wedding or religious feast.

9. Pair of skin bags with decorative fringes, blue beads and shirt buttons, Jordan. The larger bag (*mijrabat al-gahweh*) is for storing coffee beans, and the smaller one for cardamom seeds (*hayl*) which are used to give bedouin coffee its distinctive bitter flavour. Sometimes these bags are made from gazelle skin and called *ẓabīyeh* (pronounced *dhabīyeh*) meaning a female gazelle. Formerly these bags were ornamented with cowrie shells. L 80cm. 1975 AS3 11 (British Museum).

10. Ladle (*miḥmāṣeh*) and stirrer (*yad*) of iron with applied decoration, Aleppo, Syria. Used for roasting coffee beans over the fire (see cover). L 78cm. 1975 AS7 17a and b (British Museum).

11. Wooden dish (*mabradah*), Jordan. Coffee beans are put to cool in a dish after they have been roasted. This example is most unusual in form, apparently representing a lizard-like creature with the head as handle, three legs, and the open spout (through which the beans are poured into the mortar) as the tail. This piece forms part of a set with the mortar, pestle and lid illustrated in Plates 12 and 13. L 44cm. 1974 AS29 15 (British Museum).

12. Mortar (*nijir* or *mihbāsh*) and pestle (*yad*) of wood with applied white metal decoration, Jordan. Used for pounding the coffee beans after they have been roasted and cooled. The pestle is knocked against the inside of the mortar in a rhythmic beat. This announces that fresh coffee is being prepared and that guests have probably arrived. Coffee mortars and pestles are carved by craftsmen in the villages in the wooded hilly areas of Jordan and Syria and are used by both bedouin and settled villagers. Terebinth (*buṭm*) is thought to be the most suitable wood both for its resistance to cracking and its resonance when beaten.
H of mortar 28cm, L of pestle 82cm.
1974 AS29 14a and c (British Museum).

13. Wooden stopper for the mortar illustrated in Plate 12. Used to prevent the inside of the mortar becoming dirty when not in use.
H 24cm. 1974 AS29 14b (British Museum).

14. Brass coffee pot (*dalleh*) with stamped decoration and maker's name, Syria. Most tents possess at least three coffee pots, one for boiling water and cooking the coffee, the others for adding the cardamom, keeping the coffee warm and serving. Most coffee pots used in north Arabia are made in Damascus and Aleppo in Syria.
H 32cm. 1971 AS2 4 (British Museum).

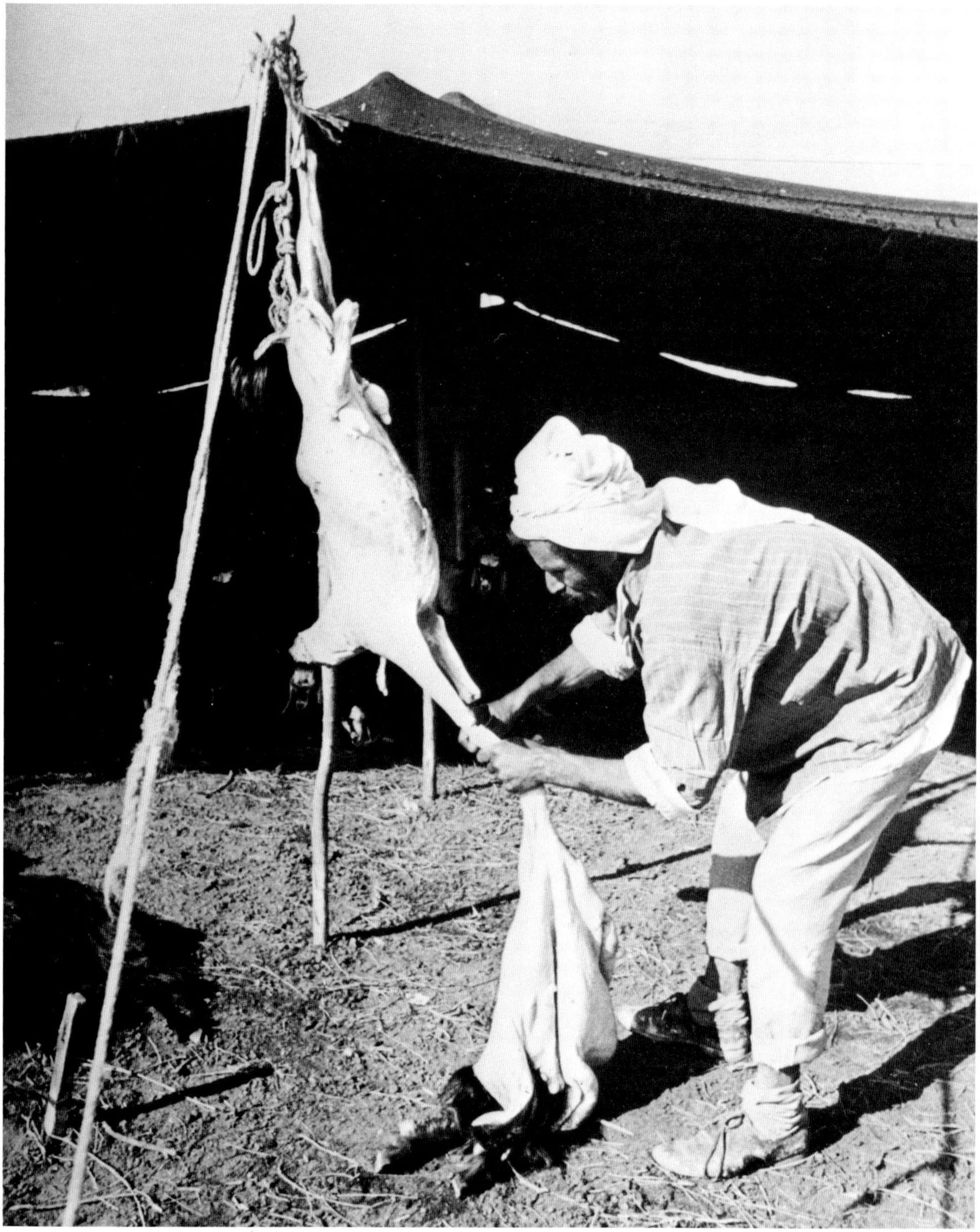

15. Skinning a goat, ʻAzāzmeh bedouin, Negev desert. Meat is a luxury food and animals are slaughtered only for festive occasions or when special guests are to be entertained. This goat is being slaughtered on the occasion of *ʻĪd al-Aḍḥā* (an important Muslim festival). Goatskins are used for various purposes foremost of which is the storage of certain foodstuffs – clarified butter (*saman*) and sour milk (*laban*) – and the transport and storage of water.
Photo: Shelagh Weir 1974.

Fig. 4. Cooking pot *(gidr)* of copper lined with tin, made in Syria. H 24cm. 1975 AS7 25.

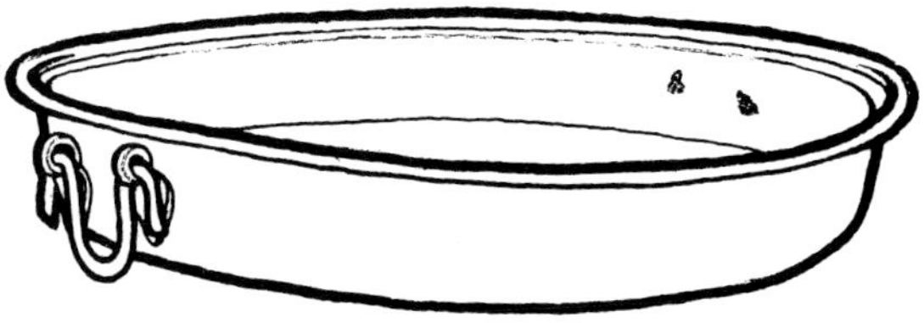

Fig. 5. Copper serving dish *(ṣaḥen)* made in Syria. D 62cm. 1975 AS7 34.

16. Men eating from a communal dish, Ibn Sha'alān (Rwāla) bedouin, north east Jordan. The dish contains twenty-four whole sheep on a bed of rice. The occasion is a grand feast given in honour of a member of the Saudi royal family for which one camel and eighty-six sheep were slaughtered. When guests are being entertained, women and children eat separately from the men. Photo: William Lancaster 1973.

17. The bedouin fiddle (*rabābah*) is often played to entertain guests.
Photo: Paul de Munter 1974.

The women's section (*al-maḥram*)

In the women's section are stored most of the utensils, bedding, food and personal possessions of the family. The bedding – rugs (*mafrash* and *bsāṭ*), mattresses (*firāsh*) and quilts (*liḥāf*) – is usually stacked in a pile against the dividing wall of the tent (Plate 5). In this pile are also bags containing clothing and other small personal possessions, and, leaning against it at the back, woven sacks (*'idl*) of grey or white wool containing grain, flour, cheese and other foodstuffs. Along one wall on a bed of stones will lie a row of goatskin bags (*girbeh*), some containing water, others clarified butter (*saman*) and, in spring, yoghurt (*laban*). Cooking pots and other utensils will be scattered around a fireplace, and there might be part of a loom intruding into the tent so the weaver can work in the shade of the roof. In some tents special sleeping compartments (*manāmeh*) are made by suspending a woven curtain (*sāḥah*) from the tent poles to form little rooms (Plate II). These are filled with bedding and cushions and make cosy nests for the family to sleep in, as well as affording a degree of privacy. A special rectangular room (*khullah*) is also constructed for a bridal couple from a red woollen rug.

A bedouin woman has many responsibilities and works very hard. It is her job, unless she can delegate it to a child, to fetch water from the nearest well and transport it back to camp on a mule or a camel in large containers (*rāwīyeh*), now made from car tyres but formerly made from camel skin. She has the everyday task of cooking for the family and, in spring, milking the animals. Erecting and dismantling the tent is also mainly women's work (Plate 3). Weaving is the hardest job a bedouin woman has to do, and many weave their entire tent, and the bags and rugs in it. As well as all these tasks she has to take care of the children, and attempt to keep the tent in order – a difficult job when dust from the desert is constantly blowing in and children are playing all around.

Making bread

Among a woman's most important accomplishments is the ability to make the large thin unleavened bedouin bread (*shirak*). The grain is bought in the villages or towns. The grains are first sifted in a circular sieve (*ghurbāl*), with a wooden frame and leather thongs (bought in the towns), then ground on a stone rotary quern (*irḥah*) (Plate 19), although many bedouin buy their flour ready milled. A little salt is added to the flour and it is kneaded and pummelled in a bowl with water until it gains the right consistency (Plate 20). (Formerly the bowls used for this were made from wood (*bāṭiyeh*) but these are no longer made as aluminium bowls have replaced them. The bowl illustrated in Fig. 6 was clearly treasured by its owner judging by its many patches.) Then pieces are torn off the dough and patted into small cakes on a floured tray or mat (Plate 18), and shaped for cooking. This operation requires the greatest dexterity and skill. Each cake is patted back and forth between the palms of the hands so that it quickly grows thinner and increases in size. When it reaches a diameter of about 50 cm it is thrown onto an iron baking tray (*sāj*) sitting on three stones over a fire (Plate V). It is turned over once and is so thin that it cooks in a matter of seconds.

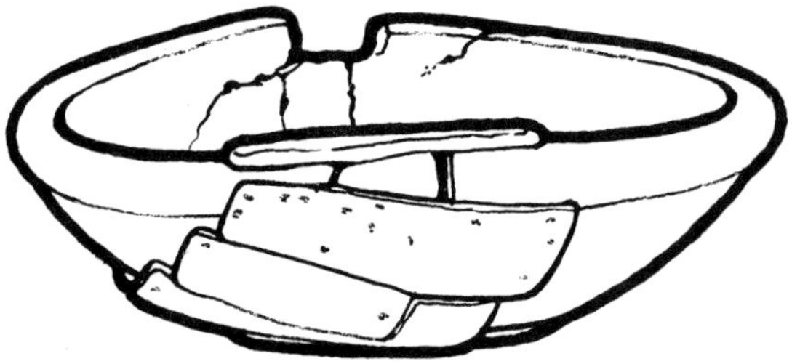

Fig. 6. Wooden bowl (*bāṭiyeh*) for mixing dough.
D 47cm. 1975 AS7 24.

18. Breadmaking in Jordan showing the wooden bowl (*bāṭiyeh*) used for kneading the dough before aluminium vessels were used. The woman is flouring the pancake of dough in a dish (*ṣaḥen*) while the flat pancake of bread (*shirak*) cooks on a domed metal tray (*sāj*) (see also Plate V and Fig. 6). Photo: Matson, 1920–48.

19. Woman of the ʻArab al-Hayb bedouin, Galilee, grinding grain on a granite rotary quern (*irḥah*).
Photo: Shelagh Weir 1968 (© British Museum).

20. Woman of the ʻAzāzmeh bedouin, Negev desert, kneading dough for bread. She is wearing bracelets (*maṣrīyeh*) similar to those illustrated in Plate 78.
Photo: Klaus-Otto Hundt 1975.

Milk products

Milk products are, with bread, the most important staple food among the sheep and goat herders of south Jordan. The season for milk is the spring. The animals are milked after they return from pasture in the evening, usually by women (Plate 21). Some of the milk is drunk fresh, but most of it is turned into yoghurt (*laban*). To make yoghurt the milk is brought to the boil in a cooking pot, until recently of tinned copper (*gidr*) (Fig. 4), allowed to cool, and left overnight either in the pan with some *laban* from the previous day to provide the necessary bacteria, or in a skin bag which contains enough of the culture from the previous day to turn the milk to yoghurt. Some yoghurt is kept for immediate consumption. It is a great treat for visitors to bedouin tents in the spring to be offered a drink from a bowl of *laban* richly flavoured with the herbs and grasses of the lush spring pastures. Most of the yoghurt is set aside to be treated in one of two ways to conserve it for consumption throughout the rest of the year.

One method of preservation is to turn it into clarified butter (*saman*). The yoghurt is placed in a goatskin (*sa'an*) which is suspended from a tripod and shaken back and forth for one or two hours (Plate IV). At intervals the neck of the skin is opened and the woman blows into it (which is said to help the butter to form). Churning is one of the

21. Woman milking a goat at dusk, south Jordan. Photo: I. G. Dunn 1975.

more welcome of women's chores. The work is not strenuous and they can chat to their friends at the same time. When the butter (*zibdeh*) has formed it is removed and boiled in a pan with a number of spices. These give the clarified butter a delicious flavour. It is then stored in goatskin bags in the women's section to be used in cooking.

The other method of preserving milk is to turn it into cheese (*jamīd*). The *laban* is boiled then poured into a fabric bag (*kīs*) to drain. Afterwards it is put in a skin bag, salt is added and it is kneaded until it hardens. Then it is removed and formed into small balls which are put on to the tent roof to dry in the sun (Plate 22). When the cheeses have become very hard they are put away in sacks. *Jamīd* can be nibbled when dry, but normally it is reconstituted, for cooking, by being sieved into hot water. *Saman*, *jamīd* and *laban*, in season, are used in cooking the traditional dish of *mansaf* – mutton served on a bed of rice and bread (*shirak*) (Plate 16).

Further information on bedouin domestic life can be obtained from the following sources: Ashkenazi (1938: pp. 122–129), de Boucheman (1935), Dalman (1928–42), Dickson (1949: pp. 84–107 and 189–201), Freer (1924), Jaussen (1908: pp. 64–74) and Musil (1908 and 1928b).

22. Balls of salted goats' cheese (*jamīd*) drying on the roof of a tent, south Jordan.
Photo: I. G. Dunn 1975.

Transport

It is the camel which has enabled the bedouin to occupy the inner deserts and steppes of Arabia. Despite the advent of the motor vehicle it is still of the greatest importance as a riding and pack animal to the sheep and goat herders of the desert fringes, and to the camel herding tribes of the interior.

A variety of harness can be fitted over the hump of the camel: light racing saddles, ordinary riding saddles (Plate 28), pack saddles, and various types of litters (Plate 23) for women to sit in when travelling, and for brides at the time of a wedding. Many bands and trappings are woven for camels both for functional and decorative purposes (Plates 24, 32 and 33). A special trough (Plate 26) is carried when travelling to enable camels to be watered at wells.

The horse, like the camel, was used in the past in inter-tribal feuding and raiding, but in recent years its importance has been primarily for use in falconry and sporting pursuits (Plate 34). Horse trappings are not made by the bedouin themselves, but by specialist craftsmen in the cities of Syria.

23. 'Ajman bedouin with camels carrying all their belongings, Saudi Arabia. The large wing-shaped litters (*ketab*) are for women, and are often highly decorated. One camel is carrying two troughs (see Plate 26).
Photo: W. H. I. Shakespear 1911 (© Royal Geographical Society).

24. Section of a woollen band (*libab*), Jordan. Red wool with multicoloured patterned sections in twined weft weave, and tassels ornamented with blue glass rings. Long bands such as this are used in the Negev desert, Jordan and Saudi Arabia to decorate the camel and litter on special occasions such as weddings.
L 11m 76cm.
1975 AS7 3 (British Museum).

25. Watering camels and donkeys, and filling water skins, at the wells of al-Hinna, Saudi Arabia.
Photo: W. H. I. Shakespear 1911
(© Royal Geographical Society).

26. Camel trough (*ḥoḍ*) with legs of bent wood and bowl of camel skin. H 72cm, D 90cm.
Photo: Shelagh Weir (Palestine Folk Museum Collection).

27 Camel and rider in the Negev desert. The saddlebag is in twined weft weave and the rider is resting his right leg on the fringed leather cushion (*mirakah*) lying on the front of the camel's hump. Photo: Shelagh Weir 1974.

These and related subjects are discussed in many articles and books on the bedouin, including the following: Allen (1975), de Boucheman (1934: pp. 35–76), Dickson (1949: pp. 409–446 and 379–398), Dostal (1959 and 1967), Field (1952), van Gennep (1902), Jennings-Bramley (1900), Johnstone (1961), Musil (1928b: pp. 329–370 and 371–388), Raswan (1945), Sweet (1965a and b) and Tweedie (1961).

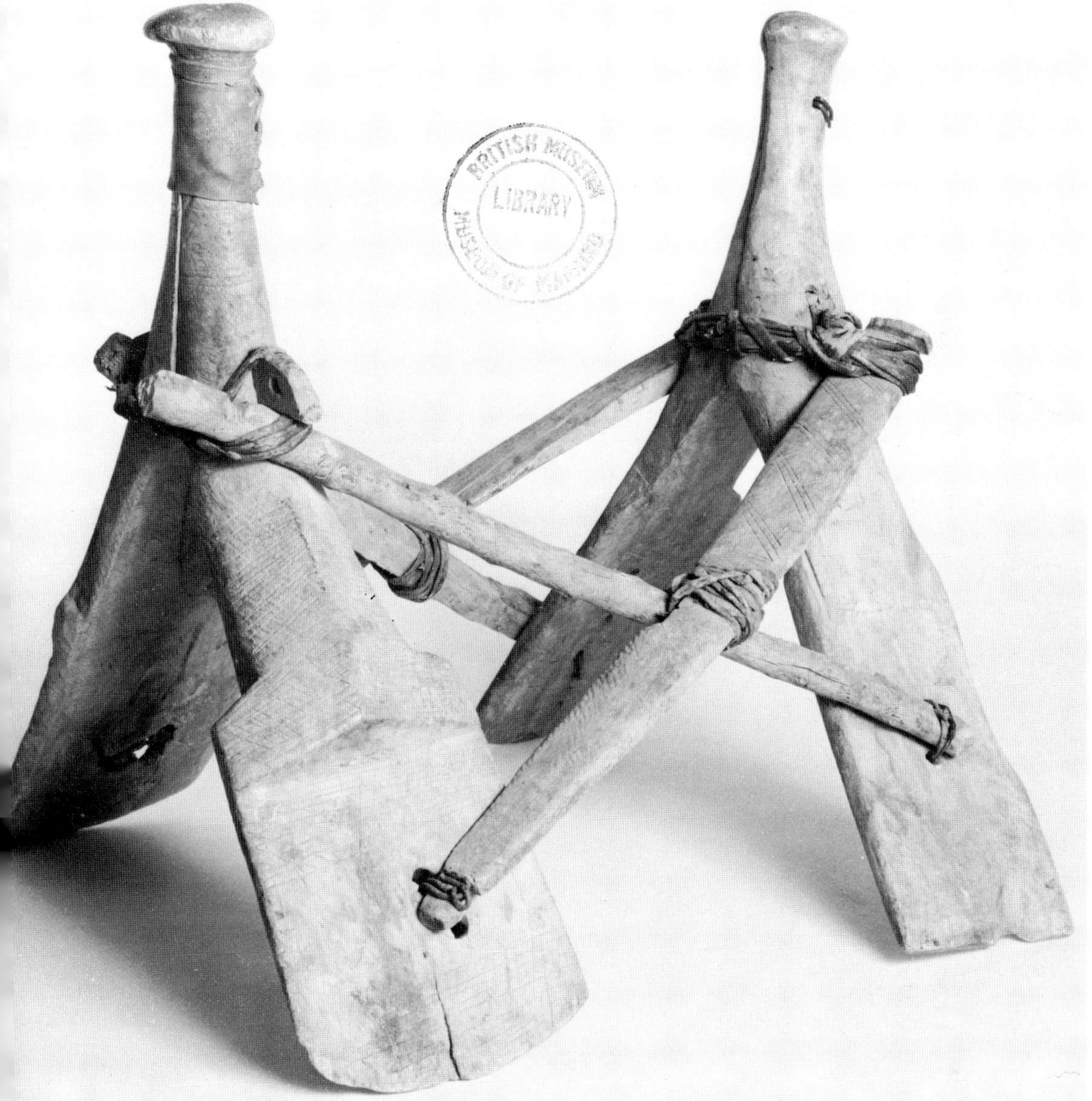

28. Camel riding saddle (*shdād*) of wood lashed with leather thongs, Jordan. The saddle is tied to the camel with woven, sometimes decorated, bands which pass under the belly. Normally a woven blanket is placed over it first, then the saddlebag, the pommels projecting through slits in the fabric, and lastly a sheepskin to make a soft seat for the rider. Saddles are made by the bedouin themselves, or by craftsmen in the villages of the wooded, hilly areas bordering the desert.
L 51cm, W 48cm, H 51cm. 1974 AS29 17 (British Museum).

29. Leather cushion (*mirakah*) placed on the front of the camel's hump for the rider to rest one of his legs on. Jordan. W 50cm.
1974 AS29 4 (British Museum).

30. One end of a camel saddlebag (*khurj*) in twined weft weave in red, blue, orange and white wool with centre section in goat hair and white wool plain weave.
L 270cm, W 60cm. 1974 AS29 5 (British Museum).

31. Camel with elaborately fringed saddlebag in twined weft weave, Wadi Rum, south Jordan.
Photo: Shelagh Weir 1974.

32. Camel decoration (*mirakah*), Jordan. Twined weft weave in red, orange, pink, blue and black wool and white cotton. Placed on the front of the hump, instead of a leather cushion, for the rider's leg to rest on.
W 75cm. 1971 AS1 37 (British Museum).

33. Headstall (*rasan*) for a camel, Jordan or Negev desert. Multicoloured wool in twined weft weave, and decorated with blue beads, cowrie shells, buttons and coins.
L 74cm. 1971 AS1 43a (British Museum).

34. Bedouin hunter on horseback with his falcon, Jordan. The saddlebag is in twined weft weave. The rider is wearing the thick headropes (*'agāl*) fashionable in the early part of this century. Photo: Matson, 1920–48.

Weaving

The following account of bedouin weaving is based on observations among various groups of the Ḥuwayṭāt tribe in south Jordan, mainly the Bani Na'īmāt, Dhiyabāt and Ibn Jāzī. A number of woven articles from Syria and the Negev desert have been illustrated, in addition to Jordanian pieces, for comparative purposes. Bedouin weaving is of special interest for a number of reasons. The tents and other goods essential to the bedouin are woven, weaving is the only developed craft among the bedouin and the medium for their only decorative art (apart from embroidery), and the craft is entirely in the hands of the women.

35. Man shearing a sheep, 'Azāzmeh bedouin, Negev desert. Shearing is normally a man's job, whereas all the other processes in textile production among the bedouin are the responsibility of women. Photo: Klaus-Otto Hundt 1975.

36. Woman spinning wool by rolling the shaft of the spindle on her thigh, south Jordan. In the Jordan/Palestine area, the spinning is always done to the right. (See also Plate VIII). Photo: Shelagh Weir 1975.

37. Spindle (*maghzal*) with goat hair yarn and a prepared rove of hair, south Jordan.
L 48.5cm.
1975 AS9 8 (British Museum).

Bedouin weaving has been described in any detail only by Crowfoot (1945), Dalman (1928: Vol V) and Peters (1952). De Boucheman (1934: p. 116) illustrates a Sba'a loom but the drawing contains several inaccuracies. These mistakes were perpetuated by Dickson (1949: p. 98) who appears to have copied the drawing, though he does not acknowledge the source. Some Arabic terms are provided by Musil (1908 Vol 3: pp. 124–5 and 1928b: p. 68) and Jaussen (1908: p. 32), who relegates the subject to a footnote. It seems that the terms used for the parts of the loom vary according to locality or group, but further studies are needed before comparisons between different groups can be made on this or any other aspect of the craft.

Spinning

After shearing has taken place (Plate 35), the goat hair and wool are teased by hand ready for spinning. The fibres are spun with a simple hand spindle (*maghzal*) consisting of a wooden shaft, and a wooden whorl, made from a single bar or crossed bars, with a metal hook projecting above it (Plate 37). They are thus similar to those used by the villagers in the Judean Hills (Weir 1970: p. 10), except that the shafts appear to be somewhat longer.

38. Woman of the Bani Na'imāt bedouin, south Jordan, standing before a tent draped with newly dyed wool drying in the sun. Wool is usually dyed in the yarn with dyes bought in town markets, or taken to dying shops to be dyed by specialists. Formerly the bedouin used natural dyes. Photo: Shelagh Weir 1975.

Before spinning, the fibres are teased with the fingers into a long *rove* twisted slightly in the direction of spin. During spinning the rove is wrapped round the left wrist or allowed to float cloud-like over the left shoulder (Plate 36). No distaff is used to hold the rove. The distaff does not appear to have been used by either the settled peoples or the nomads of north Arabia, though I have observed its use among the bedouin in Qatar and the villagers of Yemen. The method most often used for spinning is with the spindle suspended, sometimes called the drop-and-spin method. The thread is caught under the hook above the whorl, and the spin is achieved by rolling the shaft of the spindle on the thigh from the knee upwards, or twirling the whorl in the fingers in a clockwise direction. The spindle is then dropped spinning, whorl uppermost, while the thread is drawn out from the rove with the fingers. When a length of thread has been spun, it is unhooked, wound round the shaft of the spindle then hooked up again. The direction of spin is always to the right: Z-spun. According to Crowfoot (1945) this is the direction of spin throughout the Syro-Palestine area including Jordan, whereas in Egypt and the north Sudan it is to the left, S-spun. This geographical difference in spinning technique also appears to have existed in antiquity. I did not observe the spinning of cotton, though the Ḥuwayṭāt women said they spun their own cotton thread from raw cotton which they bought in Maʿān market. According to Crowfoot (1945) cotton was spun by the Bani Ḥasan in north Jordan with the spindle whorl downwards, and the spindle was not dropped, but simply rolled on the thigh as the thread was drawn out from the rove.

The spun thread is wound off the spindle shaft into skeins and dyed if a coloured yarn is required (Plate 38). Then it is rolled into a ball, and rewound into balls of doubled thread ready for plying. Two-ply yarn (*mabrūm*) is used for both the warp and the weft in bedouin weaving. Plying is done with a spindle, apparently the same as that used for spinning (called *mabram* instead of *maghzal* when thus used). When plying, the woman usually sits on the ground, and either rotates the spindle shaft on her thigh with one hand while drawing out the doubled thread from the ball with the other, or holds the thread high to allow the spindle to rotate in the air (Plate VIII). The direction of spin for plying is, of course, to the left.

The loom *(naṭi)*

A loom is a device for maintaining the *warp* threads in tension while the *weft* thread is interwoven with them at right angles. The bedouin loom fulfills this function with a minimum of simple components, namely a number of sticks and beams only one of which, the *sword beater*, is carved for the purpose. The apparatus is specially set up each time something is to be woven, and dismantled when it is completed.

Before weaving, the warp threads are stretched between two *warp rods* of iron or wood (I did not observe this). The distance between the warp rods, that is the length of the loom, depends on the desired length of the item to be woven, and the width required decides

39. Loom and tent of the Bani Naʿimāt bedouin, south Jordan. (See Plate IX where the same loom is illustrated in colour.) Photo: Shelagh Weir 1975.

40. Weaving on the bedouin ground loom (*naṭi*), south Jordan. Pushing down on the warp threads to obtain the shed. Photo: Shelagh Weir 1974.

the number of warp threads. The warp rods are lashed to beams, a *warp beam* and a *breast beam*, which are pegged firmly into the ground. It is very important that the warp threads be of even tension. As the warp is continuous, one long thread having been wound back and forth round the warp rods, the tension can be adjusted more easily than if each thread were tied to the rods separately. After warping, the warps are divided into two sets of alternate threads. One set, which I will call the *heddle warps*, is suspended from a *heddle rod* by means of a continuous *leash*, and passes under a *shed stick*. The other set, which I will call the *shed stick warps*, passes over the shed stick. The shed stick thus separates the two sets of warps, and they cross between the shed stick and the heddle rod.

Three basic weaving processes take place on all looms, changing the positions of the different sets of warp threads to form the *shed* and *countershed* (Fig. 8), inserting the weft thread, and beating-in the weft thread. Many hand looms have mechanical apparatus which relieve the weaver of some of the hard work of performing these tasks. The bedouin loom has no such mechanical aids. Its operation though simple in theory is extremely arduous in practice, depending for its effectiveness entirely on the physical strength and manual dexterity of the weaver.

The weaving process

The weaver sits at one end of the loom facing the heddle. As weaving progresses she sits on the woven fabric, thereby helping maintain the loom in tension. The weaving process involves interchanging the two sets of warp threads lying immediately in front of her. The heddle on the bedouin loom holds one set of warp threads permanently at a fixed height, and is *never* moved up and down in the vertical plane during weaving to create the shed and countershed. The warp threads can only be alternated by the physical exertions of the weaver, and the operation requires strength because the rough-spun threads cling together and are heavy to handle. Fig. 7 shows the warps forming a shed. To obtain the countershed, the shed stick warps must be raised above the heddle warps. Reaching over the heddle, the weaver pulls the shed stick towards the heddle, then grasps handfuls of the shed stick warps and tugs them upwards, at the same time pushing down on the heddle warps. Gradually she raises the shed stick warps above the heddle warps on her side of the heddle. Gathering the shed stick warps on one arm, she inserts the sword in the flat position in the newly-formed countershed, and, grasping each end, pulls it towards her to complete the separation of the two sets of warps and to force the 'crossing' down to the edge of the woven fabric. The sword is then turned on edge to keep the countershed open while the weft thread is passed through (the *pick*). To return the warp threads to the shed position the weaver first removes the sword, then presses down with the flat of her hand with all her weight onto the warps on her side of the heddle. She then leans over the heddle and presses down on the warps on the other side, forcing the shed stick warps down to their former position. The result is to return the 'crossing' to the far side of the heddle. As before, the sword is inserted

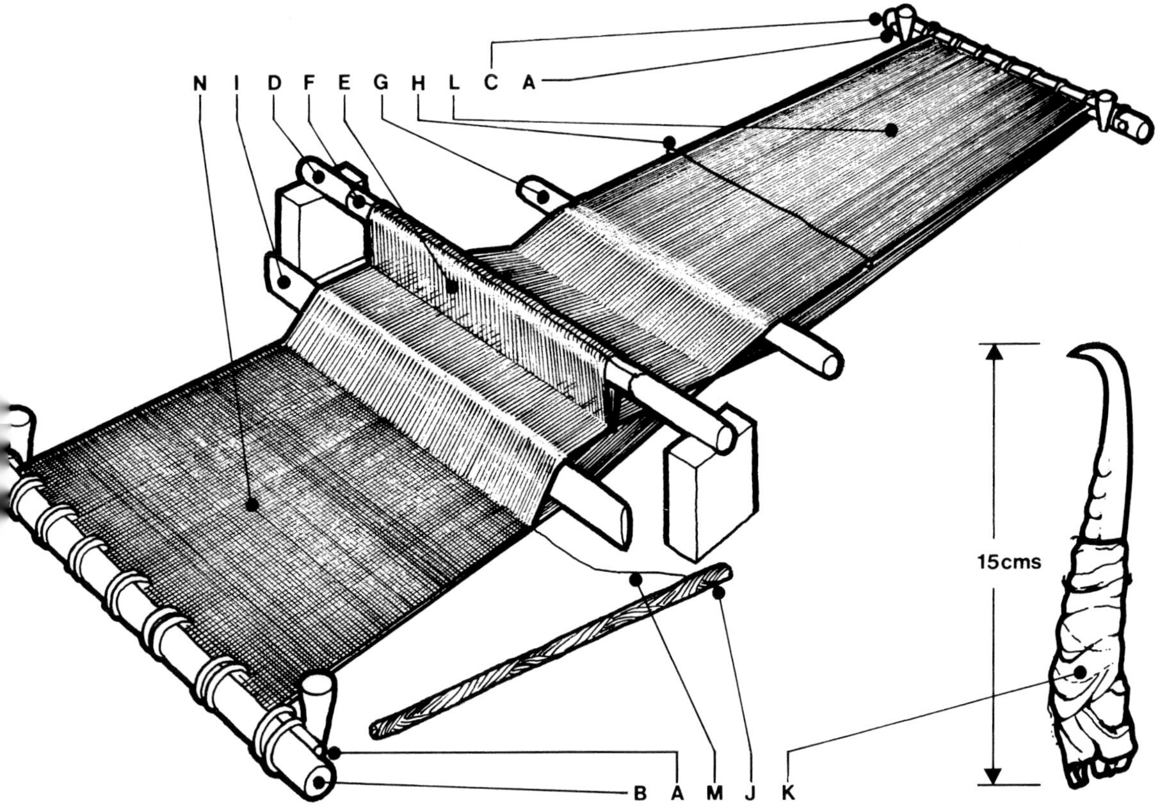

Fig. 7. The bedouin loom (*naṭi*): terms used for the various parts of the loom among the Ḥuwayṭāt bedouin, south Jordan.

A	warp rod	*muṭrag*
B	breast beam	*gāʿ al-naṭi*
C	warp beam	*ras al-naṭi*
D	heddle rod	*minyār*
E	leashes	*nīreh*
F	string securing leashes	*gaṭar*
G	shed stick	*ḥāf, maḥāfah*
H	string round upper warps	*gilādeh*
I	sword beater	*minshāz, minsāj, minḥāz*
J	stick spool	*maysha'*
K	beating hook	*mishgā, miḥtā*
L	warp threads	*sitā*
M	weft thread	*laḥmeh*
N	woven fabric	

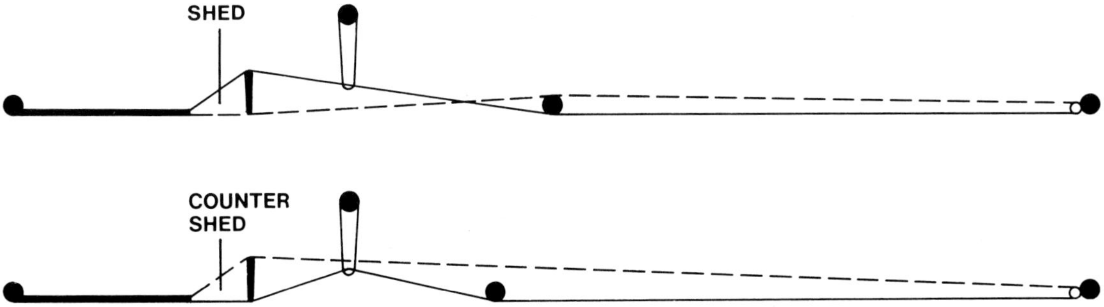

Fig. 8. Shedding diagram of the bedouin loom (not to scale).

into the newly formed shed to complete the separation of the warps, then turned on edge for the pick. As well as using the sword to separate the threads, the weaver also strums them from side to side with her beating hook, and prods them with her outstretched fingers. Some weavers also rub a bar of soap across the warps to make their separation easier.

A pick is made, that is the weft thread is passed through the shed or countershed, by means of a simple *stick spool* (equivalent in function to a shuttle on a more sophisticated loom). The spool can be any stick about one metre long, and the weft is wound onto it in long figures-of-eight. The weft is unwound from the spool before each pick. The main implement for beating-in the weft thread is the *beating hook*, either a steel hook or a gazelle horn (Fig. 7K). It is used as follows: the weaver inserts the sword on its edge between the upper and lower warps, and pulls it up close to the fabric. This tautens the upper warps and presents them at a more convenient angle to the weaver. With the hook she then plucks up groups of these upper

41. Weaving on the bedouin ground loom, south Jordan. Pulling up the shed-stick warp threads to obtain the countershed. Photo: Shelagh Weir 1975.

warps, then beats down with force towards the fabric. This plucking and beating movement is done very quickly in a series of deft movements, from one side of the loom to the other, two, three or four times, to drive the weft firmly home. As the hooks weigh very little, the success of the beating-in depends entirely on the strength of the weaver and the dexterous way she manipulates the hook.

The sword beater is usually considered to be the main implement used for beating-in on this type of loom, but in south Jordan this is not the case, and sometimes it is not used at all for this purpose. When it is, the narrow edge is beaten against the fabric with force one, two or three times before or after beating-in with the hooks.

Weaving practices vary according to personal preference or the type of fabric required. Thus beating-in may be more rigorous when a close weave fabric, for example a tent roof, is required, or less rigorous when an item is being made for sale. Also some weavers beat-in immediately after making the pick, others change the shed first and then beat-in, and others do both.

As the woven section grows the heddle rod has to be moved, with its supports, along the loom. Sometimes when a very long piece of cloth is being woven, such as a tent roof strip, the breast beam is released from its pegs, part of the woven section is rolled up, and the warp rod and beam are anchored again. This makes it easier to keep the loom in tension and to protect the woven part from the sun or rain.

The maximum width is limited to that which two weavers working together can manage, that is up to about one metre. When an article is required that is wider, two loom widths are joined together lengthways. Such widths are usually woven in sequence along the same warp: accounting for the frequent failure to match the designs

42. Weaving on the bedouin ground loom, south Jordan. Beating-in the weft thread with gazelle horns. Photo: Shelagh Weir 1974.

on a patterned article (Plate IX). Looms can extend to twelve or more metres in length.

The fabrics

Most fabrics woven by the bedouin are in plain weave. For this, single alternate warp threads pass through each of the leash loops and weaving takes place as described above. The finished fabric is *warp faced*, that is the weft is concealed after beating-in and only the warp is seen. Some plain weave fabrics have stripes and bands of colour. This is achieved by using coloured threads for the requisite number of warps. Because the fabric is warp faced, these show up as coloured bands in the final product. The bedouin also weave quite complex and extremely attractive patterns into their fabrics. The patterns are achieved by the use of two different techniques of weaving: one giving a warp faced pattern and the other a weft faced pattern. These types of pattern weaving are unknown among the village women of the Judean hills and north west Jordan, who use a similar loom. However, both techniques are widespread among the bedouin in Arabia.

Warp patterns *(ragm)*

Warp faced patterns are worked in bands running lengthways on the loom and therefore on the finished article (see Plate IX). For this type of patterning each leash loop carries two warps instead of one, one of the pattern colour, which is most often white, and one of the background colour, for example black. The warps lying over the shed stick are arranged in pairs likewise. The warps for the plain weave sections adjacent to the pattern bands pass singly through the leashes in the normal way. To make the pattern the weaver selects with her fingers one thread from each pair of warps (at the shed or countershed position), leaving the other one to float as a loose strand on the back of the fabric until it is selected to appear on the surface as part of the design (Plate X). As the required warps are selected, the sword is pushed through to keep them separate while the next pattern band, if there is one, is worked. When each of perhaps two or three pattern bands have been worked in this way, the selected warps are threaded onto the weaver's arm while the shed of the plain sections is changed, then the sword is pushed through and turned on edge to keep the threads separate for the pick. The weft is passed through on the spool and beaten-in as in plain weaving. Examples of this type of weaving are illustrated in Plates 43, 44, 45, 46 and 51.

Twined weft patterns *(nagash)*

Weft faced patterns are usually worked in bands at intervals across the width of a plain weave fabric. To make this type of pattern the weaver uses two strands of weft thread at a time and with the fingers inserts one under, and the other over, each warp thread (Plate XI). Sometimes the wefts are passed over and under two, three or even more warps at a time. The technique is essentially the same as that used in twined basketry. When a straight sided design is worked, a slit tapestry effect results, but usually the designs are diamonds and shapes with sloping edges so that the weft can overlap and long slits are avoided. The weft is beaten-in as for plain weave. Examples of this type of weaving are illustrated in Plates 24, 30, 32, 43, 47 and 50.

43. Section of a tent dividing curtain (*sāḥāh* or *gāṭa'ah*), Jordan or Syria. Five strips are joined lengthways, and the curtain includes examples of the two different pattern weaving techniques used by the bedouin.
Top strip: red wool with tassels W 9cm.
2nd and 3rd strips: dark blue wool with white cotton warp patterns W 23cm and 48cm.
4th and 5th strips: black goat hair with pattern bands in twined weft weave in red, blue, green and white wool.
W 51cm and 50cm.
This is a particularly fine curtain of the type often made specially as a gift from one tribal shaykh to another. It is possible that the warp patterned strips and the twined weave strips were made separately, and by different tribes, and joined together by the final owner. The warp patterned strips are Syrian in style, and include figurative designs of human figures and camels. The strips with twined weave designs could be Syrian or Jordanian.
Total L 10m (British Museum). Presented by H.R.H. Sherif Nasser Bin Jamil.

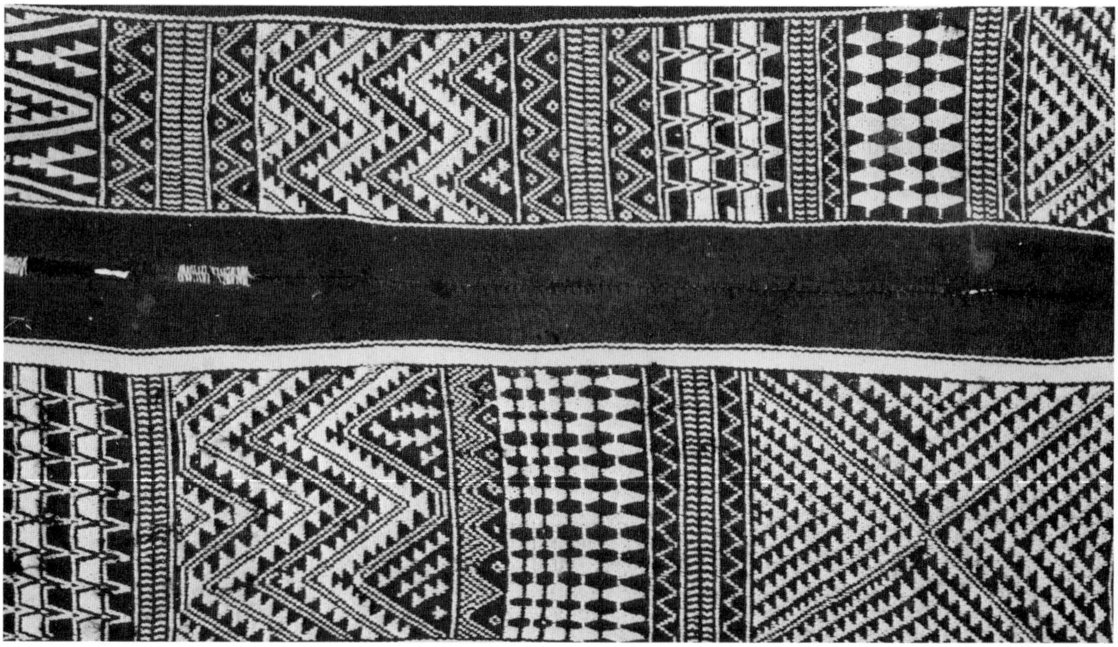

44. Section of a dividing curtain (*sāḥah*) for a tent, possibly Ḥuwayṭāt bedouin, Jordan. Woven from black goat hair with white cotton warp patterns. A third strip of plain woven wool, about 40cm wide, is attached below these two patterned strips. This type of richly patterned curtain was made and used by certain Jordanian tribes up to twenty or thirty years ago, but is now no longer made and rarely seen (see Plate 56).
W of top section 43cm and lower section 70cm. Total L 7m 30cm.
1974 AS29 3 (British Museum).

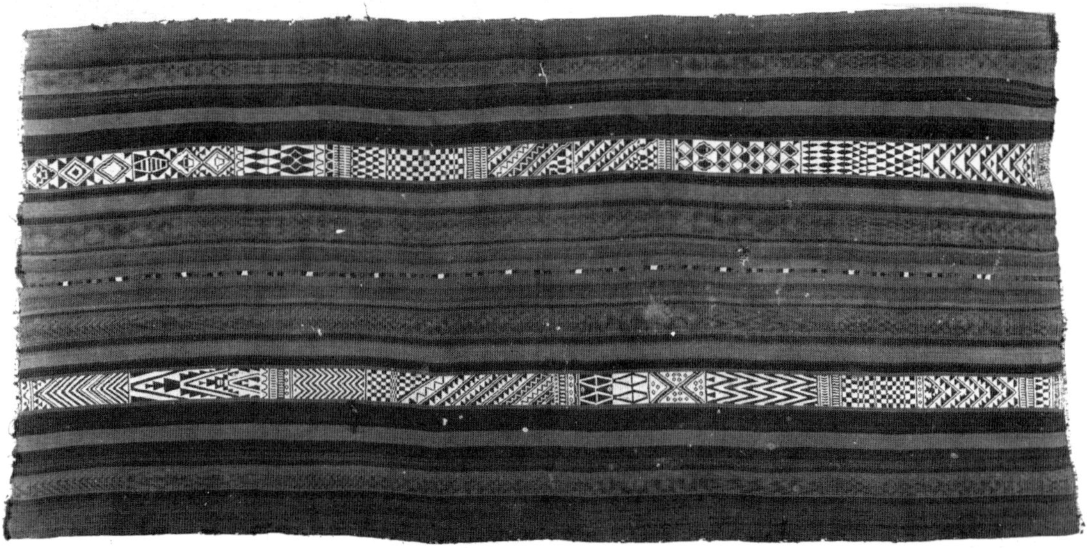

45. Rug (*bsāṭ*), probably Ḥuwayṭāt bedouin, south Jordan. Woven in green, brown and red bands of wool, with warp patterns in white (cotton) on brown, and red on green. Two loom widths are joined lengthways. (Compare with that being woven in Plates IX and 39).
L 287cm.
1975 AS3 7 (British Museum).

46. Storage and travelling bag (*'idl*), Syria. Red and white warp patterns on a dark blue background. All wool including the white. The bag is made from two loom widths joined lengthways, folded and sewn up the sides with coloured wools. The tasselled fringe in red, orange and yellow wool may have been added separately to make the bag more festive for a special occasion such as a wedding. Bags such as this are used to store possessions in the tent, and in pairs, one on each side of a camel when travelling.
W 114cm. 1975 AS7 4 (British Museum).

Plaiting

In the Negev desert and Jordan, girdles (*gīsh* and *shwaḥīyeh*) were formerly made by a technique which combined plaiting and weaving. The threads were plaited towards the centre and the outer strands became 'wefts' as each in turn was woven through the other threads (Plates 48 and 49). This process and its distribution is well described by Crowfoot (1943).

47. Section of a rug (*bsāṭ*), Dhiyabāt bedouin, south Jordan. The background is in brown and white bands of wool, and the transverse pattern bands in twined weft weave in red, orange, dark and light blue and white wool. Two loom widths are sewn together lengthways.
Total L 3m 65cm.
1974 AS29 6 (British Museum).

48. Two ends of a woollen girdle (*gīsh*), Negev desert. Plaited in black with narrow V-shaped stripes in red, blue and green. One end is in multicoloured twined weft weave and decorated with tassels, and beads of bone and blue and brown glass. The other end is decorated with cowrie shells. This narrow girdle is wrapped around the waist over a wider belt made from narrow plaited strips of black goat hair and white wool sewn together to make a band about 10cm wide.
W 3.5cm and 8cm, L 288cm.
1974 AS29 26 (British Museum).

49. Woman of the Tarābīn bedouin, Negev desert, plaiting a girdle (*gīsh*) (see Plate 59).
Photo: Grace Crowfoot 1920's or 30's (© Elizabeth Crowfoot).

Weaving products

The most important product of the bedouin loom is the cloth for their tents. The strips from which the roof of the tent is sewn are made from goat hair, or a mixture of goat hair and wool. In the latter case, the warp is goat hair and the weft is wool, or wool and goat hair plyed. The front and back walls may contain more wool than the roof which needs to be stronger and more waterproof. The back wall often has one or two decorative bands of white cotton.

The most splendid item woven for the tent is the dividing curtain (*sāḥah*). Dividing curtains with intricate geometric warp patterns were widespread among the tribes of Jordan and Syria until about thirty years ago (Plates 43 and 44). Musil (1908, pp. 129 and 162) illustrates two examples among the Ibn Fāyez bedouin in south Jordan. Crowfoot (1945) mentions seeing them among the Ghanamāt bedouin near Madaba, and Bani Ḥasan bedouin near Jerash. I have seen them in several tents of the Na'īmāt in south Jordan (Plate II). The women lament that this type of weaving is on the decline.

Among the Ṭuwayḥā bedouin near Bayyīr in south east Jordan, I saw dividing curtains in white cotton with small pattern bands in the twined weft technique (similar to the lower part of the curtain illustrated in Plate 43). The dividing curtains used by the various tribes throughout Arabia would make an interesting study. In Qatar large decorative panels of twined weft are woven at one end of the curtain, and in the Empty Quarter warp patterns are worked on curtains and other textiles (Cole: 1975 pp. 81–82).

Apart from tent cloths, the bedouin women weave rugs (*mafrash* when plain, *bsāṭ* when patterned) (Plates 45 and 47), saddle-bags (*khurj*) for camels and horses (Plate 30 and back cover), storage sacks (*'idl*) (Plate 46), bags (*mizwad*) also used as cushions (Plates 50 and 51), and trappings for camels and horses (Plates 32 and 33).

Textiles produced for the bedouin by town and village weavers

Many bedouin are unable to make for themselves all the textiles they need or want. The camel herding tribes of the inner deserts do not have the goats and sheep to provide the hair and wool for their tent cloth, rugs and bags. Also some women are unable to weave because they lack the skill or the time. Sometimes tent cloth is needed quickly, for example when a man wishes to marry and set up his own tent at short notice. In such cases the cloth has to be bought ready made. One solution is to buy from other bedouin who have made surplus to their own requirements. Therefore one cannot assume that any piece of weaving was actually made by the women of the tent or tribe where it is found. Fine pieces of weaving such as dividing curtains (*sāḥah*) undoubtedly pass from hand to hand and are given as presents (Plate 43).

50. Cushion cover (*mizwad*), probably Negev bedouin. Woven in twined weft weave in red, blue, white, orange, yellow and green wool. Used for storing small possessions in the tent, and as a cushion for guests to lean on.
L 80cm. 1975 AS3 4 (British Museum).

51. Cushion cover (*mizwad*), Syria. Woven in wool in black with a dark red stripe, and warp patterns in white.
L 102cm. 1975 AS7 6 (British Museum).

52. Weaver, Aḥmad Yasin Hajj Shehādi, in Irbid, north Jordan, weaving a strip for a tent wall (*ruwāg*). Vertical fixed-heddle looms such as this are used by male weavers in certain towns and villages in Jordan, Lebanon and Syria (and until 1948 in Palestine) to weave the cloth for the walls and roofs of bedouin tents. The cloth is made on commission, or is sold in the local markets, for tribes from as far afield as Saudi Arabia and the Gulf. The demand is mainly from the camel herders who have insufficient goats to make their own cloth, and from those bedouin whose women cannot weave, or who need the cloth urgently. Photo: Shelagh Weir 1974.

The main external sources of textiles for the bedouin are the towns and villages of the settled areas bordering the deserts. Here a weaving industry exists which is based partly on the demand from the bedouin for textiles they are unable to provide for themselves. The weavers are always men, and work on two different types of loom, a vertical loom with a fixed heddle, and a horizontal loom with moveable heddles.

It is on the vertical loom that cloth for the roofs and walls of bedouin tents is produced. Dalman (1937 Vol. V: p. 107), Crowfoot (1941) and Weir (1970) describe the workings of this loom. Vertical looms manufacturing tent cloth were in widespread use in Palestine during the British Mandate (1920–48), and looms were operating in Safad, Majd al-Kurum, Samakh, Beisan, Anabta, Tulkarm, Nablus and Hebron. The vertical loom has not been used in the Palestine area since about 1948. Cloth for the bedouin of southern Palestine was also made in the big weaving centre of Shiḥīm in southern Lebanon. (Abū Muḥammad, a weaver now working in Jerash, related how he used to travel from Shiḥīm, to sell his cloth to the Negev bedouin in Rafah, Khan Yunis, Gaza and Beersheba in Palestine during the British Mandate.) When this market was cut off in 1948, many weavers moved to Syria and Jordan. The weavers working today in Irbid and Jerash in Jordan are originally from Shiḥīm. In Syria, the vertical loom industry is still in existence, according to informants, in Yabroud, Riha, Homs, Damascus, Latakia and Tartous.

The hair and wool for the vertical looms is provided locally by goat and sheep herders, both villagers and bedouin, and it is also imported from Egypt and Libya. It is spun and plyed simultaneously on an ingenious hand spinning apparatus similar to that used in the Balkans. The cloth is woven mostly on commission, though if he can, the weaver will make surplus for sale in the markets. Customers of the Jordanian weavers include nomads from as far afield as Saudi Arabia, Qatar, Abu Dhabi, Dubai, Iraq and the Sudan. Usually the customers or traders come to place their orders directly with the weavers.

It is interesting to note here that in north Yemen male weavers use a fixed heddle ground loom, similar in most respects to that of the bedouin women, to make tent cloth for the bedouin (Weir: 1975).

Mention should also be made of the horizontal treadle loom industry (Weir 1970: p. 27). Rugs made by male weavers working on this type of loom in Madaba, in Jordan, and many towns in Syria, are traded all over Jordan and bought by the bedouin for use in their tents.

53. Bedouin of Palestine wearing a voluminous sleeveless cloak (*'abāyah*) of striped woven wool, made in the cities by male weavers and worn by the bedouin of north Arabia. A similar cloak of finer wool or cotton without stripes, and with metal thread embroidery at the neck, is worn by shaykhs and others for special occasions. Early twentieth century.

Costume

All the fabrics used for clothing are purchased from itinerant merchants or from the markets in towns, and clothes are often bought ready made. The traditional costumes of both men and women are well adapted to the extremes of temperature in the desert. They are loose fitting with several layers providing good insulation. Clothing can denote social or marital status, and a woman's clothing often indicates the tribe or locality from which she comes. To illustrate this regional variation I have included descriptions and pictures of women's costume from the Galilee area and the Negev desert as well as Jordan. It appears that the style of bedouin women's costume is usually influenced by that of the village women in the same locality. Propriety demands that both sexes maintain a modest appearance and keep the head and most of the body covered, but in the Levant area few bedouin women are obliged to cover their faces.

Further information on bedouin costumes in the area can be obtained from the following sources: Ashkenazi (1938: pp. 130–140), de Boucheman (1934: pp. 11–34), Jaussen (1908: pp. 32–34 and 52) and Musil (1928: pp. 115–131).

Women's costume

Until about thirty years ago, the bedouin women of the east side of the river Jordan, then Transjordan, wore an extraordinary dress of enormous proportions. It was three metres long and had long pointed 'wing' sleeves up to two metres in length (Plate 55). In the nineteenth century and early this century this dress was made from blue machine-woven cotton, but later black cotton became the fashion. This was not the dress of a giantess, as one might suppose, but was a combination of dress, underdress and veil. A girdle (*shwaḥīyeh*) of plaited wool was tied over the dress and around the waist, and the material was pulled up and through the belt until the hem was level with the ground and the excess material fell in a baggy fold. This fold was called the *'ob*, and the dress was called *thōb 'ob* or *khalakah* (Plate 56). The points of one or both sleeves were thrown over the head as a veil, and secured with a band (*'aṣbeh*), often, for best wear, of fine brocaded silk. Sometimes the dress had some simple embroidery in zig zag lines (*'irayjeh*) on the front. This dress must have been comfortable in all weathers with the different layers insulating the body against heat or cold. However, women say they liked it 'because it hid the body well'. Similar dresses are still worn by some of the older women of al-Salt and Jericho today, the latter embroidering the front with narrow vertical bands in gaily coloured cross stitch. The bedouin women of Jordan no longer wear the *thōb ʻob*, but prefer dresses of normal size in satin and man-made fibres. However, the pointed sleeves still survive in a rudimentary form: set into the dress inside-out, turned back on themselves and joined between the shoulder blades. A colourful print dress with long tight sleeves is worn underneath. The head is covered with a gay nylon scarf.

The costumes worn by the bedouin women of the Palestine area (now Israel) are very different from those worn east of the river

54. Woman of the ʻArab al-Hayb bedouin, Galilee, embroidering a panel for the skirt of a dress (*shursh*). She is wearing a black crepe head veil (*milfaʻ*), a silk and metal brocade head band (*ʻaṣbeh*) and gold coins (British sovereigns) round her forehead. Photo: Shelagh Weir 1968 (© British Museum).

Jordan. In the Negev desert the women's dress was, until recently, of black cotton with long pointed sleeves, and richly embroidered in cross stitch in a manner similar to and probably influenced by the dress of the village women of the Judean hills (Plates 57 and 58). Bedouin embroidery reflects a woman's marital status. Red embroidery, which is the favourite embroidery colour, can only be worn after marriage, and unmarried girls can only wear blue embroidery (Bailey: 1974b). On their heads, girls wear a bonnet (*uggā*) of silk (*aṭlas*) ornamented with coins. Married women sometimes wear a band (*burgaʻ*) ornamented with coins which partly covers the face

55. The 'double dress' (*thōb ʻōb*) of Jordan. This giant-sized dress was worn by the bedouin and settled peoples of south Jordan during the last century and the first part of the twentieth century, and is still worn by some of the older women of the town of al-Salt today. The excess material was pulled through a belt so as to hang over in a fold (*ʻob*) above the hem of the dress.
Photo: Shelagh Weir 1968 (© British Museum).

(Plate 79). Over the head is worn a black cotton veil edged with red cotton appliqué, or a black cloak (*'abāyah*). The girdle (*gīsh*) is plaited in grey and black wool (Plates 48 and 49). On festive occasions the women wear a number of gay woven bands (Plate 60) suspended from their belt, and embroidered tasselled decorations (*garāmīl*) on their plaits.

56. Woman of the 'Adwan bedouin, Jordan, wearing the 'double dress'. She is standing before the patterned dividing curtain (*sāḥah*) of her tent. One of the long sleeves of the dress is pulled over her head and secured by a head band (*'aṣbeh*).
Photo: Matson, 1920–48.

57. Dress (*thōb*) worn by the bedouin of the Beersheba area, Negev desert. Black cotton with cross stitch embroidery in multicoloured silks. The embroidery of this area is strongly influenced by that of the village women of south Palestine in its designs and its distribution on the dress. Before European embroidery silks came on the market, red was the predominant embroidery colour for married women, and blue for unmarried women. Today machine embroidery is superseding hand embroidery.
L 153cm, Maximum W 128cm.
1971 AS1 8 (British Museum).

58. Back skirt panel of the dress illustrated in Plate 58.

The costume worn by the bedouin women in Galilee is also similar to and possibly influenced by that of village women, in this case that of the Remtha area of north Jordan. The dress (*shursh*) has long tight sleeves and a panel of running stitch embroidery in a band above the hem (Plate 54). The embroidery is executed in the 'negative', that is the designs are made by the black material showing through between the stitches. Thirty years ago the embroidery cotton was white and gave a lace-like effect. Today it is usually multicoloured. The head is covered with a black crepe veil (*milfa'*), which is draped so as to cover the neck and chest, and secured by a red or purple silk headband (*'aṣbeh*) with metal thread brocade (Plate VII). In winter a jacket (*dāmer*) of black cotton (formerly of woollen broadcloth), with red embroidery, is worn over the dress.

59. Woman of the *'Azāzmeh* bedouin, Negev desert, wearing a plaited woollen girdle (*gīsh*) decorated with cowrie shells (see Plates 48 and 49).
Photo: Klaus-Otto Hundt 1975.

60. Decorative bands, Negev desert. Multicoloured wool and white cotton in twined weft weave. A number of these bands are suspended from their belts by the women of the Beersheba area for festive occasions.
Maximum L 71cm.
1975 AS7 9, 10 and 11 (British Museum).

Men's costume

Until about the middle of this century the traditional costume of bedouin men throughout the Palestine/Jordan area consisted of a long white robe (*thōb*), a wide sleeveless cloak (*'abāyeh*), a head veil (*keffīyeh*) and head ropes (*'agāl*) (Plate 53). (At the beginning of the century the head ropes were much thicker than they are today.) Over the *thōb* a leather cartridge belt, or a tablet woven belt (*gmār*), made in Damascus, was worn. For special occasions a long sleeved coat (*gumbāz*, *kibber*) of satin (*aṭlas*) was worn over the *thōb*. The cloak for everyday wear was woven from wool and often striped (Plate 53). Cloaks of cotton or fine wool were worn in summer. A man of high status would wear a cloak of fine quality camel hair or silk cloth embroidered round the neck with metal thread, headropes with sections of silver or gold thread, and an elaborate silver dagger (Plate 61). A coat (*furwah*) of broadcloth lined with fleece was also worn in winter (Plate 62).

61. Young bedouin shaykh wearing head ropes (*'agāl*) ornamented with metal wire, and a dagger decorated with niello patterns. Palestine, early twentieth century.

62. Man wearing the fleece-lined winter coat (*furwah*) made in the cities and worn by the bedouin in winter.
Photo: William Lancaster 1973.

ıt and loom of the Bani Naʿīmāt bedouin, south Jordan. Photo: Shelagh Weir 1974.

:eping compartments (*manāmeh*) in the women's section of a tent of the Bani Naʿīmāt bedouin, south Jordan. Photo: Shelagh Weir 1975.

III. Pounding coffee beans in a wooden mortar (*mihbāsh*), south Jordan. Photo: Shelagh Weir 1974.

IV. Churning butter in a goatskin (*sāʿan*) suspended from a tripod, Bani Naʿīmāt bedouin, south Jordan. Photo: Shelagh Weir 1975.

ing bread (*shirak*) on a convex metal tray (*sāj*), Bani Na'īmāt bedouin, south Jordan. Photo: Shelagh Weir 1975.

VI. Woman with tattoos and dress with embroidered chest panel, Negev desert.
Photo: Shelagh Weir 1968 (© British Museum).

VII. Woman of the 'Arab al-Hayb bedouin, Galilee.
Photo: Shelagh Weir 1968 (© British Museum).

Plying woollen thread to make a two-ply yarn for weaving. Bani Na'īmāt bedouin, south Jordan. Photo: Shelagh Weir 1975.

IX. Weaving a warp patterned rug (*bsāṭ*), Bani Na'imāt bedouin, south Jordan. Photo: Shelagh Weir 1974.

ecting the warp threads to make the pattern on a rug (*bsāṭ*). Photo: Shelagh Weir 1975.

XI. Weaving a rug (*bsāṭ*) with twined weft patterned sections, Dhiyabāt bedouin, south Jordan. Photo: Shelagh Weir 1974.
XII. Weaving a panel (*shuggah*) for the roof of a tent, Ibn Jāzi bedouin, south Jordan. Photo: Shelagh Weir 1975.

Jewellery

A bedouin woman appreciates jewellery for its ornamental value, but it is also important to her in other ways. She normally acquires her first jewellery collection at marriage and it remains an outward sign of her new marital status. It also represents her own share in her marriage transaction. Her jewellery is either part of the brideprice paid by the groom to her father, or is bought for her by her father after he receives the brideprice. In either case, the jewellery is entirely her own property. If she needs cash she can sell part of it, or if she earns money she can add to it. In this way she can bank her capital in a portable commodity which has intrinsic value, and which experience has shown will keep its true worth. Also, certain pieces of jewellery are thought to have protective and beneficial effects on the wearer, and particularly popular among bedouin women is jewellery which combines talismanic with decorative functions.

The bride is never involved in the purchasing of the jewellery, and may not even know that her marriage is about to take place. Bedouin camped near a town visit the silversmith's shop to buy the jewellery, while those camped in the desert buy from itinerant craftsmen and traders who travel round the bedouin camps with their wares. Formerly gypsies (*nuwār*) made a living in this way.

All the jewellery illustrated here was fashionable among the bedouin women of the Palestine/Jordan area during the first half of this century. Similar styles may have been worn in the nineteenth century and earlier, but we have no means of knowing. Every town had its silversmiths who made the jewellery for all the people in their locality. Where there is a mixed population of townspeople, villagers and bedouin, they would all wear similar jewellery produced by the same silversmiths. The main differences would be in the value of the pieces. As bedouin were usually poorer than the settled peoples, the silversmiths provided for them cheaper items of lower grade silver.

The jewellery styles of this area have been subjected to many influences. Jewellery brought back from the Ḥajj and imported by Christian and Muslim pilgrims must have been the source of many new ideas. Other innovations in technique and design were brought in by foreign silversmiths who were attracted by the relative prosperity of the Levant. Many of the silversmiths working in Transjordan and Palestine early this century were from outside: Syrians, Hejāzis, Armenians, Circassians and Yemenites. It is also interesting to note that silversmiths were often members of religious minorities: Christians or Jews. Two of the jewellery techniques in use during this period are remembered as having been introduced by foreign silver-

63. Yusef Faghāl, a silversmith who came to Jordan from Medina, Saudi Arabia, with the Emir Abdullah's expedition in 1921. He worked in Madaba, Amman and Kerak, where he now lives, and was one of the craftsmen responsible for introducing Hejāzi techniques and styles of jewellery to Jordan.
Photo: Shelagh Weir 1974.

Fig. 9. Bracelet (*asāwir sirkez*).
D 6cm.
1975 AS3 46.

smiths. In the 1920's jewellery decorated with soldered pieces and granulation appeared. This technique is said to have been brought to the area by a group of Hejāzi silversmiths who came to Transjordan with the Emir Abdullah in 1921 (Plate 63). Later, jewellery decorated with black enamel (niello) became very popular and this technique is attributed to the Circassian and Armenian silversmiths who settled in Transjordan from the late nineteenth century onwards. Bracelets with niello decoration are still called *asāwir sirkez*, meaning 'Circassian bracelet', in south Jordan (Fig. 9). The reason given for the great popularity of niello is that the customer could be sure that jewellery was made from a high quality silver if it had niello decoration because the enamel would not take on a low grade metal. Filigree work probably came originally from Yemen. There were a number of Yemenite Jewish silversmiths working in the Jordan area long before the mass exodus of Jews from Yemen in 1950. Silversmiths were

64. Small charms (*ḥijāb*) worn by children and adults to protect them from dangers and illnesses.
Left: Red stone inscribed with Arabic script, set in silver with silver pendants and coins.
Centre: Blue ceramic bead set in silver with silver pendants.
Right: Light brown bead, possibly amber, with shallow incised markings, set in base metal with pendant base metal imitation coins and a figure resembling a frog. Many stones and beads are thought to have particular powers. For example, the blue bead is thought to provide protection against the evil eye, red stones to ensure good health and a milky white stone to promote successful lactation in nursing mothers.
L 9cm, 10cm and 7cm. 1971 AS1 79, 81 and 78 (British Museum).

extremely jealous of their technical expertise and the secrets of their craft were closely guarded within their families.

In the later 1930's silver jewellery began to go out of fashion and was replaced by gold, a process which seems to have taken place more gradually in Transjordan than in Palestine. The reason for this change can be understood in the context of the social and economic importance of jewellery. During the period of British rule the area

65. Small charms (*ḥijāb*).
Left: a silver rosette in the centre of which a blue bead, against the evil eye, was probably mounted.
Right: the tooth of an animal mounted in silver. Certain animals' teeth and bones are thought to give protection against misfortune.
L 6cm and 10cm.
1971 AS1 83 and 1975 AS3 50 (British Museum).

66. Amulet (*māskeh*) of silver, inscribed with the name of Allah. Attached to the chain are two tubular silver boxes (*khiyārah*, literally 'cucumber'). Such containers are often called amulet cases, although they rarely contain anything. Said by one silversmith to have been made in al-Salt, Jordan, by a Syrian craftsman.
L 33cm, D of amulet 5.5cm.
1975 AS3 25 (British Museum).

became more prosperous. Goods became more expensive, the bride-price rose along with other prices and the value of the bridal jewellery rose proportionately. At the same time, the old sources of silver – Maria Theresa dollars and Turkish riyals – dried up, and gold became more easily available. Few of the silversmiths seem to have been able to adapt to the new material, and the manufacture of gold jewellery became centred in the cities: mainly in Damascus and Beirut. The interaction between the ideas and talents of the individual craftsman and the tastes and needs of the customer disappeared, and gold jewellery was mass produced in uniform styles. Today all the younger bedouin women wear gold jewellery, or gold coins strung on a ribbon round their necks or on a band round their foreheads (Plate VII). Many of the older women have now sold their silver and exchanged it for gold.

67. Amulets (*māskeh*) of hammered silver with incised decoration and Arabic script, some very crudely applied. Amulets such as these were made by itinerant silversmiths who visited bedouin camps and worked and sold their wares on the spot.
L 6cm, 5cm and 6cm.
Top: 1971 AS1 68.
Bottom: 1975 AS3 23, 21 and 20 (British Museum).

68. Amulets (*māskeh*) of silver with niello decoration, and pendant sand-cast ornaments and coins. Worn round the neck on silver chains, these amulets were fashionable among the bedouin women in Jordan until twenty or thirty years ago. Made by jewellers in Kerak, Amman and Irbid.
L 21–13cm.
Left-right: 1971 AS1 71 and 70 and 1975 AS3 18 (British Museum).

Fig. 10. Detail from a silver chain (*jnād*).
Total L 108cm.
1975 AS3 16.

69. Amulet (*ḥijāb*) in the form of a rectangular box in silver with niello decoration, and pendant sand-cast ornaments and coins. The chain also has sand-cast ornaments at intervals. These boxes are often called amulet cases, but there is usually only wadding inside. Made in Jordan and worn round the neck by the bedouin women up to twenty or thirty years ago.
L inclusive chain 55cm, L of amulet 12.5cm.
1971 AS1 66 (British Museum).

70. Amulet (*ḥijāb*) in the form of a fish, Jordan. Silver with relief decoration made by the sand-casting technique from an original made by the filigree technique. The diamond shaped ornaments may have been applied after casting. The baubles attached to the chain are probably a later addition. The eye socket would have contained a blue bead (against the evil eye). The decoration of this piece shows Hejāzi influence, and it was probably made by one of the Hejāzi jewellers such as Yusef Faghāl (Plate 63) or his predecessors.
Length 8cm. 1975 AS3 17 (British Museum).

Techniques

The following techniques for working silver were in use among the silversmiths of the Palestine/Jordan area during the first part of this century.

Hammering (*ṭariq*)
The silver is hammered into flat sheets then cut and/or bent to the required shape, and soldered as necessary. This technique is often combined with engraving (Plates 66 and 67).

Repoussé (*ḍarab shakūsh*): a sheet of silver is laid on a bed of pitch and hammered with variously shaped punches, or it is hammered onto a shaped mould. In either case the design appears in relief on the reverse side of the work (Plate 77).

Filigree (*qisr shift* or *mshabak*)
Qisr shift roughly translated means 'forced with pliers' and *mshabak* means 'netted'. Filigree is the twisting and soldering together of wire to make various patterns. This technique is commonly used for baubles and relief decoration on a plain or engraved silver base (Plates 70 and 75).

71. Amulets (*samakah*) in the form of fishes, Jordan. Silver with niello decoration, the centre amulet with sand-cast pendant ornaments, the others with pendant coins. The fish is a very old decorative motif in the Middle East. Although it may once have been a fertility symbol, when asked, neither the women who wore these ornaments during the 1920's and 1930's nor the silversmiths who made them, attributed any special significance to the shape.
Length of fish 8–9.5cm. 1971 AS1 73, 74 and 72 (British Museum).

Granulation (*shughl al-khurduq* or *habbīyāt*)
The soldering (*talḥīm*) of small silver granules, or other shapes, particularly diamonds, onto a silver base. When the granules are in clusters they are called 'mulberry seeds' (*habbāt al-tūt*). This technique is often combined with filigree work (Plates 65, 70 and 75).

Sand casting (*sakib*)
A mould is made by pressing the model between a pair of iron frames packed tightly with very fine sand (*raml*). The sand is treated with a mixture of alum, salt and sugar in water so as to retain the exact impression of the model when it is removed. A copy is then cast from this mould (which can be used only once). This technique can be used to copy pieces made by any of the other techniques (Plates 68, 69, 70, 73 and 76).

Enamelling or niello (*mḥabar*)
Mḥabar derives from the word for ink and refers to the black colour of the enamel. The powered enamel is placed in etched or cast recesses in the silver ornament, then melted and filed to make a smooth surface (Plates 68, 69, 71 and 80).

Chainmaking
A variety of chains (*sinsāl*) were made, with different types of links, spacers and baubles combining the techniques of filigree, granulation and sandcasting (Plates 69, 70, 71 and Fig. 10).

The main source of silver was coins: Maria Theresa dollars (called *abu rīsheh*, literally 'father of feathers' because of the wings depicted on the obverse) which contained about eighty percent silver, Turkish riyals which had a lower silver content, and base metal coins for cheap jewellery. The best quality jewellery contained about eighty percent silver. The main alloy used was copper which was said to give the best sheen.

72. Necklace (*gilādet al-krunful*), Negev desert. A choker of various kinds and colours of beads, and pendant from it three multiple strings of cloves interspersed with beads, coral and mother-of-pearl spacers. The strings terminate with blue, maroon and orange silk tassels, each strand ending in a tiny glass bead.
L 53cm.
1975 AS3 31 (British Museum).

The jewellery

The following items of jewellery were worn by bedouin women throughout the Jordan area up to the 1940's, and were made by silversmiths working in Irbid, Amman, Madaba, al-Salt and Kerak.

Amulets

(a) Stones and beads, sometimes set in silver. Many colours and types, each one effective against a particular ill. For example, a bottle green stone (*kharazet al-kabseh*) against post-natal disease in a mother, a smooth white stone (*kharazet al-ḥalīb*) to promote lactation in nursing mothers, and a blue bead (*'owayneh*) against the evil eye (Plates 64 and 65).
(b) Oval in shape (*māskeh*). Plain hammered silver with engraved patterns or Quranic inscriptions (Plate 67), and with niello decoration (Plate 68).
(c) Rectangular boxes (*ḥijāb*) with niello decoration (Plate 69).
(d) Cylindrical boxes (*khiyārah*) (Plate 66).
(e) Fish-shaped amulets (*samakah*), filigree, sand cast or decorated with niello (Plates 70 and 71).

73. Necklace (*kirdān*), Jordan. Silver ornaments attached to a textile band, and silver sand-cast ornaments and coins pendant from it. Made in Irbid, Kerak and Nablus (Palestine) up to about twenty years ago, and worn by both bedouin and village women.
L of neckband 32cm. 1975 AS3 15 (British Museum).

Necklaces

(a) Chains (bedouin: *jarīr*, townspeople: *sinsāl*). Various kinds: links with floral ornaments at intervals (*sinsāl farkeh*), rods at intervals (*sinsāl 'amūd*), and with baubles and balls attached (*jnād*) (Fig. 10). Some very long, reaching to the waist, some worn under one arm, and others shorter with amulets pendant from them.

(b) Choker (*kirdān*), silver ornaments and pendants on a cotton band. Made with a variable number of silver ornaments to suit the pocket of the customer (Plate 73).

(c) Necklaces (*'oqd mirjān*) of coral with amber and mother of pearl spacers.

(d) Necklaces of cylindrically shaped amber beads.

74. Girl of the 'Azāzmeh bedouin wearing bead necklaces, hair pins decorated with coins, and a gold nose ring (*shnāf*). Photo: Shelagh Weir 1974.

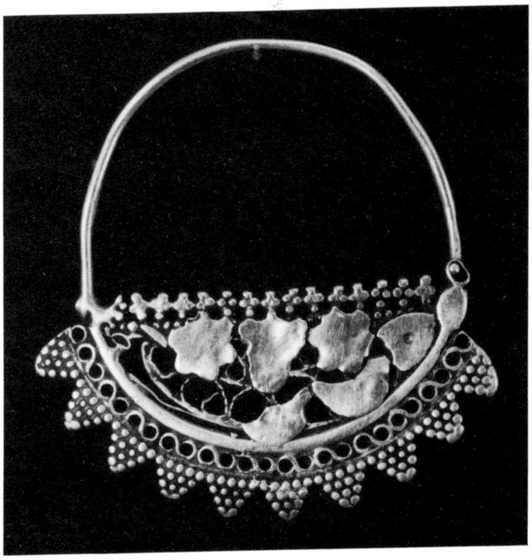

75. Gold nose ring (*shnāf*) worn by bedouin women in the Negev desert.
W 3.5cm.
1975 AS3 29 (British Museum).

Bracelets
(a) Broad or narrow with niello decoration, always worn in pairs one on each wrist (*asāwir sirkez, sirān sarsak*) (Plate 80 and Fig. 9).
(b) Shaped amber beads.

Rings (*khawātem*)
Various stones set in silver, or plain silver rings. Up to four worn on each hand.

Hairpins (*bukleh*)
Usually decorated with niello.

Forehead ornament (*kaffāt* or *khamasiyāt*)
Worn by the semi-settled bedouin of the Jordan valley area (Plate 76).

Nose ring (*zmaymah*)
Smaller than that worn in the Negev desert, usually gold.

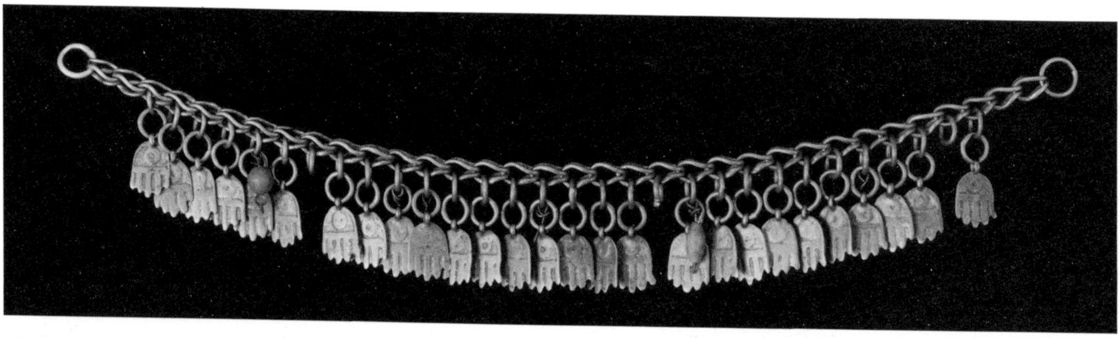

76. Ornament (*kaffāt* or *khamasiyāt*), Jordan and Palestine. Hand-shaped ornaments of low grade metal pendant from a chain. Worn around the forehead by the women of the Ta'āmreh and 'Obaydiyeh groups of semi-settled bedouin in the Jordan Valley and Bethlehem area. Made by jewellers in Jerusalem during the British Mandate period (1920–48). L 38cm. 1975 AS3 28 (British Museum).

77. Pair of silver bracelets (*saba'awīyāt*) Negev desert. Decorated in relief by the hammering technique (repoussé). One worn on each wrist. W 6.5cm. 1975 AS3 41a and b (British Museum).

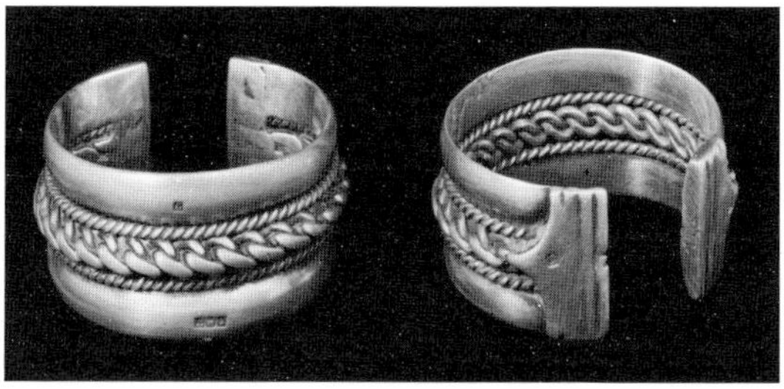

78. Pair of silver bracelets (*maṣrīymeh*), Negev desert. Made by silversmiths in Egypt (mainly Jewish). (See Plate 20.)
W 6.5cm. 1975 AS3 44a and b (British Museum).

79. Negev bedouin woman in Khan Yunis wearing a band of coins (*burga*ʻ) over her face. Coins are used as ornaments on the head and face to a greater extent in the Negev desert than in the area east of the Jordan valley.
Photo: Shelagh Weir 1967 (© British Museum).

80. Pair of silver bracelets (*asāwir mīnā*), Jordan. Ornamented with niello with a hinged opening and pin fastening. These bracelets are unusually broad and were made, according to one informant, by an Armenian silversmith called Rubīn who worked in Jerusalem during the British Mandate period.
H 6cm, W 6.5cm. 1975 AS3 48 (British Museum).

The fashions in jewellery among the Negev bedouin women were and are quite different from those in Transjordan. Most of their silver jewellery was made by jewellers in Beersheba and Gaza in southern Palestine and Cairo in Egypt. They wore pairs of bracelets (Plates 77 and 78), and favoured a great number of bead necklaces, as they still do (Plate 74). Headdresses (*uggā*) and face covers (*burga*ʿ) covered with coins were worn (Plate 79). They also wore silver or tasselled decorations on their plaits and large gold nose rings (*shnāf*, Plates 74 and 75). The bedouin women of south Jordan with their more restrained ornamentation are amused by the taste of the Negev bedouin women with their abundance of coins and other jewellery. It is possible that the latter have been influenced in the past by the villagers of southern Palestine, especially Judea, who wear a similar profusion of coins (Weir: 1973).

Bibliography

The time available for the compilation of this bibliography has been limited, and it has been impossible to look at every work to verify the entry. Annotations are given where the title does not indicate clearly the content of the publication. We have been unable to ensure, in all cases, that the transliteration of tribal names in the annotations is consistent with the system used elsewhere in this book.

Publications marked with an asterisk, ⋆ are recommended to the general reader as an introduction to the bedouin and their way of life.

The following specialist libraries, which normally require membership, hold extensive collections on this and related subjects: The Palestine Exploration Fund, 2 Hinde Mews, London W1., and The Royal Anthropological Institute, Museum of Mankind, 6 Burlington Gardens, London W1.

The following abbreviations have been used:

P.E.F.Q. and P.E.Q. Palestine Exploration (Fund) Quarterly, London

S.W.J.A. South Western Journal of Anthropology, Albuquerque

Bull. S.O.A.S. Bulletin of the School of Oriental and African Studies, University of London

J.P.O.S. Journal of the Palestine Oriental Society, Jerusalem

Z.D.P.V. Zeitschrift des Deutschen Palästina Vereins, Leipzig

Journ. R.C.A.S. Journal of the Royal Central Asian Society, London

H.R.A.F. Human Relations Area Files, New Haven

Int. Arch. für Eth. International Archiv für Ethnographie, Leiden

J.R.A.I. Journal of the Royal Anthropological Institute, London

Abou-Zeid, Ahmed M. 1968. The changing world of the nomads (Middle East, North Africa). In *Contributions to Mediterranean Sociology: Mediterranean rural communities and social change*, ed. J. G. Peristiany. Paris and The Hague: Mouton and Co.

Abou-Zeid, Ahmed M. 1965. Honour and shame among the bedouins of Egypt. In *Honour and Shame: the values of Mediterranean society*, ed. J. G. Peristiany. London: Weidenfeld & Nicholson: 243–59.

Abou-Zeid, Ahmed M. 1972. Nomadism and sedentarisation in the Arab world: a select and annotated bibliography. *Bull. of the Inst. of Arab Research Studies*, 3. March: 21–48. An unfinished bibliography of books, articles, doctoral dissertations and reports to the United Nations.

Admiralty Handbooks, see: Great Britain.

Allen, M. J. S. and Smith, G. R. 1975. Some notes on hunting techniques and practices in the Arabian Peninsula. In *Arabian Studies*, ed. R. B. Serjeant and R. L. Bidwell. London: C. Hurst. 108–147.

Amiran, D. H. K. and Ben-Arieh, Y. 1963. Sedentarisation of bedouin in Israel. *Israel Exploration Journal*, 13 (3).

Anati, Emmanuel 1956. Rock engravings from the Jebel Ideid (southern Negev). *P.E.Q.*: 5–12. On tribal marks (*wasam*).

Arab League 1965 'Idārat al-shu'ūn al-ijtimā'īyah wa'l-amal. In *Ri'āyat al-badū wa tahdīruhum wa tantīnuhum.* (Arabic). Cairo. ('Settlement and housing of bedouin'). Essays presented at the ninth conference in Jerusalem.

Ariam, Abdul Jabbar 1963. Communities, class system and caste in Iraq. *Bull. of the College of Arts, Univ. of Baghdad*, 6: 1–22. On the social mobility of urban, rural and bedouin groups.

Ariam, Abdul Jabbar 1965. *Al-qabā'il al-ruḥḥāl fi'l-'Irāq.* (Arabic). Baghdad. On the nomads of Iraq.

al-'Ārif, 'Ārif 1934. *Tārīkh bīr al-sabā' wa qabā'ilihā.* (Arabic). Jerusalem. ('A history of Beersheba and its tribes'). Selected passages translated in *P.E.F.Q.* 1937–38.

al-'Ārif, 'Ārif 1944. *Bedouin love, law and legend.* Jerusalem: Cosmos. English version, with changes, of *Al-qaḍā' bayn al-badū*, (1933). A study of legal theory and practice of the bedouin of Beersheba. (Also published in German).

* **Ashkenazi, Tovia** 1938. Tribus semi-nomades de la Palestine du nord. In *Études d'Ethnographie*, Tome 2. Paris: Paul Geuther. Ethnographic survey of eighty groups in north Palestine.

Ashkenazi, Tovia 1948. The 'Anazah tribes. *S.W.J.A.* 4 (2) summer: 222–239.

Awad, M. 1954. The assimilation of nomads in Egypt. *Geographical Review*: 240–52. New York (map).

Awad, M. 1959. The settlement of nomadic and semi-nomadic tribal groups in the Middle East. *International Labour Review.* lxxix: 27–60. Geneva.

Awad, M. 1970. Living conditions of nomadic, semi-nomadic and settled tribal groups. In *Readings in Arab Middle Eastern Societies and Cultures*, ed. Abdulla M. Lutfiyya and Charles W. Churchill. The Hague and Paris: Mouton: 135–148.

'Azzawi, 'Abbās 1947–55. *'Ashā'ir al-'Irāq.* (Arabic). 3 vols. Baghdad. ('On the tribes of Iraq').

Bacon, Elizabeth E. 1954. Types of pastoral nomadism in central and south west Asia. *S.W.J.A.* 10: 44–68.

Bacon, Elizabeth E. 1958. *'Obuk, a study of social structure in Eurasia.* New York: Viking Fund Publication in Anthropology, 25. Part 8, 123–34. On tribal organization distinguishing the vengeance unit from the clan among bedouin.

Baer, Gabriel 1969. *Studies in the social history of modern Egypt.* Chicago: Univ. of Chicago: 3–16. On the sedentarization of the bedouin.

Bailey, Clinton 1975. Aspects of bedouin culture in Sinai and the Negev. In *Notes on the bedouins*, 5. Midrashat Sde-Boker, Israel.

Bailey, Clinton 1970–76. *Notes on the bedouins.* (Hebrew). Annual Publication of the School for Field Studies, Midrashat Sde-Boker, Israel.

Bailey, Clinton 1972. The narrative context of the bedouin qasidah-poem. *Folklore Research Centre Studies*, 3: 67–105. Sinai bedouin material collected on behalf of the Midrashat Sde-Boker. Jerusalem: Hebrew University.

Bailey, Clinton 1973. Poetry of the Desert. *Ariel*, 33–34: 187–199. Jerusalem: Ministry of Foreign Affairs.

Bailey, Clinton 1974a. Bedouin star-lore in Sinai and the Negev. *Bull. S.O.A.S.* 38:3:580–86.

Bailey, Clinton 1974b. Bedouin weddings in Sinai and the Negev. In *Studies in marriage customs. Folklore Research Centre Studies*, 4: 105–132. Jerusalem: Hebrew University.

Bailey, Clinton 1976. A note on the bedouin image of 'adl as justice. (To be published in *The Muslim World*?).

Bailey, Clinton and Peled, Raphael 1975. *Shivtei ha-beduim bi-Sinai.* (Hebrew). ('A survey of the bedouin in Sinai'). Tel Aviv.

Bailey, Clinton and Shmueli, Avshalom 1977. The settlement of the Sinaitic 'Ayaydeh in the Suez Canal Zone. (To be published in *P.E.Q.*?).

★ **Baldensperger, Philip T.** 1915–29. The immovable east. *P.E.F.Q.* 1915: 67; 1916: 19–26; 1922: 23–32, 63–67, 161–172; 1926: 93–97; 1929: 183–189. A series of short articles on Palestinian bedouin dress, warfare, horses and language.

Barghuthi, Omer el-Effendi 1922. Studies in Palestinian customs and folklore (1): Judicial courts among the bedouin of Palestine. *J.P.O.S.*, 2: 34–65.

al-Bayati, Ala al-Din 1971. *al-Rāshidīyah, dirāsah anthrubulujīyah ijtimā'īyah.* (Arabic). Najaf: Maṭba'at al Nu'mān. ('A social anthropological study of the Rashayda'). On a tribe part of which migrated to the Sudan and Ethiopia about 100 years ago.

Beitenholz, P. G. n.d. *Desert and bedouin in the European mind: changing conceptions from the Middle Ages to the present time.* Khartoum: University of Khartoum, Extra-Mural Studies.

Bell, Gertrude M. L. 1907. *The desert and the sown.* London: Heinemann (illus.).

Bell, Gertrude M. L. 1940. *The Arab War.* London: The Golden Cockerel Press. Confidential information on Turkish Arabia and Kuwait sent Oct. 1916–July 1917 to General Headquarters.

Ben-David, J. 1972. *The bedouin tribes in southern Sinai.* (Hebrew). Jerusalem, M.A. Thesis.

Ben-Elkanah, S. 1961. *'Arab al-Tiāhā* (unpublished). On the Tiyāhā bedouin.

Berman, M. 1967. Social change among the Beersheba bedouin. *Human Organization:* 69–76. Lexington, Kentucky (illus., map, bibliog.).

Berry, Shirley Ruth 1940. *The changing social and economic structure of the Rwala bedouins.* Harvard University thesis.

Black-Michaud, Jacob 1975. *Cohesive force: feud in the Mediterranean and the Middle East,* foreword by E. L. Peters. Oxford: Basil Blackwell (bibliog.).

Blanc, Haim 1970. The Arabic dialect of the Negev bedouins. *Proceedings of the Israel Academy of Sciences and Humanities,* 4:7, Jerusalem.

Blunt, Anne I. N. 1879. *Bedouin tribes of the Euphrates.* 2 vols. London: John Murray; New York: Harper. On the Shammar and 'Anazah tribes before western influence in the area.

Blunt, Anne I. N. 1881. *A pilgrimage to Nejd, the cradle of the Arab race.* 2 vols. London.

Boucheman, Albert de 1934a. La sédentarisation des nomades du désert de Syrie. *L'Asie Française,* 320: 140–43. Paris.

Boucheman, Albert de 1934b. Note sur la rivalité de deux tribus moutonnières de Syrie: les Mawāli et les Ḥadidiyīn. *Revue des Études Islamiques,* 8: 11–58. Paris.

Boucheman, Albert de 1935. *Matériel de la vie bédouine recueilli dans le désert de Syrie (tribus des Arabes Sba'a).* Documents d'Études, Orientales, 3. Paris: Institut Français de Damas.

Boucheman, Albert de 1937. *Une petite cité caravanière: Suhné.* Documents d'Études Orientales, 6. Paris: Institut Français de Damas. On Sukhneh, a caravan town near Palmyra, Syria, whose inhabitants are of nomadic origin.

Bouvat, L. 1921. Le droit coûtumier des tribus bédouines de Syrie. *Revue du monde musulman,* 43. Paris: Editions Ernest Leroux.

Braslavasky, John. F. 1946. The composition of the bedouin tribes of the Negeb. *Edoth* 1: 89–100. Jerusalem.

Briggs, Lloyd Cabot 1960. *Tribes of the Sahara.* Cambridge, Mass: Harvard University Press and London: Oxford University Press.

Buckingham, J. S. 1825. *Travels among the Arab tribes inhabiting the countries east of Syria and Palestine.* London: Longman.

Burckhardt, J. L. 1822. *Travels in Syria and the Holy Land.* London: John Murray.

Burckhardt, J. L. 1829. *Travels in Arabia.* 2 vols. London: John Murray.

Burckhardt, J. L. 1830. *Notes on the Bedouins and the Wahabys,* ed. Sir W. Ouseley. London: Henry Coburn & Richard Bentley. Reprint New York, 1967.

Bury, G. Wyman 1911. *The land of Uz.* London: Macmillan. On the Aden hinterland.

Canaan, Tewfik 1928. Die Azazime-Beduinen und ihr Gebiet. *Z.D.P.V.* 51: 89–118. ('The Azāzmah bedouin and their territory').

Canaan, Tewfik 1936. The Ṣakr Bedouin of Bīsān. *J.P.O.S.* 16: 21–32.

Carruthers, Douglas 1910. A journey in north-western Arabia. *Geographical Journal,* 35:225–48. London. On the Bani Ṣakhr, Rwāla and Shararāt bedouin.

Caskel, W. 1953. *Die Bedeutung der Beduinen in der Geschichte der Araben,* Köln: Oplander. ('The importance of the bedouin in the history of the Arabs').

Caskel, W. 1954. The bedouinisation of Arabia. In *Studies in Islamic Culture,* Hist. Mem. 76, ed. G. E. von Grunebaum: 36–46.

Charles, H. 1939. *Tribus moutonnières du moyen-Euphrate.* Documents d'Études Orientales, Beirut: Institut Français de Damas.

Chelhod, Joseph 1965. L'organisation judiciare chez les bédouins du Negueb. *Anthropos* 60: 1/6, 625–45. Brno.

Chelhod, Joseph 1967. Problèmes d'ethnologie jordanienne: nomadisme et sédentarisation. *Objets et Mondes: La Revue du Musée de l'Homme,* 7: 85–102. Paris (illus.).

Chelhod, Joseph 1968. Le prix du sang dans le droit coûtumier jordanien. *Revue de l'Occident Musulman et de la Mediterranée,* 5: 41–68.

Chelhod, Joseph 1971. *Le droit dans la société bédouine: recherches ethnologiques sur le 'orf ou droit coûtumier des bedouins.* Paris: Marcel Rivière.

Chelhod, Joseph 1972. Bedouins and the law. In *Actes du Colloque sur l'étude des populations sahariennes. Revue de L'Occident Musulman et de la Mediterranée,* 11: 1–181.

Clauss, Ludwig Ferdinand 1933. *Als Beduine unter Beduinen.* Freiburg im Breisgau: Herder & Co. (reprinted 1954). (illus.). ('As a bedouin among the bedouin.') Includes information on the Bani Ṣakhr.

* **Cole, Donald Powell** 1975. *Nomads of the nomads. The Āl Murrah bedouin of the Empty Quarter.* Chicago: Aldine Publishing Co.

Conder, Claude R. 1883. Arab tribal marks (*ausam*). *P.E.F.Q.*: 178–9.

Coon, Carleton S. 1952. *Caravan: the story of the Middle East.* London: Jonathan Cape (bibliog.). Classic anthropological study of the area.

Couroyer, B. 1951. Histoire d'une tribu semi-nomade de Palestine. *Revue Biblique,* 58: 75–91. Paris. On the Ta'āmre bedouin near Bethlehem.

Crowfoot, Grace Mary 1921. Spinning and weaving in the Sudan. *Sudan Notes and Records*, 4 (1): 20–38. Khartoum.

Crowfoot, Grace Mary 1931. *Methods of hand spinning in Egypt and the Sudan.* Halifax: Bankfield Museum Notes, 2nd Series: 12.

Crowfoot, Grace Mary 1934. The mat looms of Huleh, Palestine. *P.E.F.Q.*

Crowfoot, Grace Mary 1941. The vertical loom in Palestine and Syria. *P.E.Q.* Oct.

Crowfoot, Grace Mary 1944a Handicrafts in Palestine: primitive weaving (1) Plaiting and finger weaving. *P.E.Q.* July–Oct: 121–130.

Crowfoot, Grace Mary 1944b Handicrafts in Palestine: Jerusalem hammock cradles and Hebron rugs. *P.E.Q.* Jan–April: 121–130.

Crowfoot, Grace Mary 1945. The tent beautiful: a study of pattern weaving in Trans-Jordan. *P.E.Q.* Jan–April: 34–47.

Crown: Ninth Army 1942. *Handbook of the nomad, semi-nomad, semi-sedentary and sedentary tribes of Syria* (maps). Gives lists of tribes, territories and leaders. pp. iii–xv: 'The Bedouins of northern Arabia' by John Bagot Glubb.

al-Dabbāgh, Musṭafā Murād 1963. *Jazīrat al-'Arab.* (Arabic). 2 vols. Beirut. An economic and sociological study of Arabia.

⋆ **Dalman, Gustaf Hermann** 1928–42. *Arbeit und Sitte in Palästina.* 7 vols. Gütersloh: C. Bertelsman. Reprinted: Hildesheim, 1967. On all aspects of bedouin and village life in Palestine.

Daumas, General E. 1971. *The Ways of the Desert.* Transl. by Sheila M. Ohlendorf. Univ. of Texas. Gives examples of poetry and literature of the Saharan tribes.

Di Medlio, R. R. 1970. Il problèma dei nomadi in Arabia Saudiana et le sue soluzioni. *Oriente moderno* 50: 6, June: 273–9. Rome.

⋆ **Dickson, H. R. P.** 1949. *The Arab of the desert: a glimpse into the bedawin life in Kuwait and Saudi Arabia.* London: Allen and Unwin. On the domestic life of the Shammar and 'Anazah tribes, and the Muntafiq shepherd tribes and out-cast Salubbah tribe.

Dickson, H. R. P. 1956. *Kuwait and her neighbours.* London: Allen and Unwin. On the history of Kuwait with details of the tribes, especially the 'Ajman bedouin.

⋆ **Diqs, Isaak** 1967. *A beduin boyhood.* London: Allen and Unwin. Autobiographical account by a Jordanian bedouin educated in the Western tradition.

Dostal, Walter 1959. The evolution of bedouin life. In *L'antica società beduina*, ed. Francesco Gabrieli, 1959: 11–34. Rome.

Dostal, Walter 1967. *Die Beduinen in Südarabien. Eine ethnologische Studie zur Entwicklung der Kamelwirtenkultur in Arabien.* Vienna: Berger (illus.). Ethnographical study of the bedouin in south Arabia and the development of the camel herding culture.

* **Doughty, Charles** 1885. *Travels in Arabia Deserta.* 2 vols. London: Jonathan Cape. Chap. 13, 'Peace in the Desert' reprinted in Sweet (1970): 237–64.

Dowson, V. H. W. 1949. The date and the Arab. *Journ. R.C.A.S.* 34–41.

Elphinston, W. G. 1945. The future of the bedouin of northern Arabia. *International Affairs.* 21: 370–75: London.

Encyclopaedia of Islam 1913–38. (New Edition) *Badw.* London: Luzac. Includes information on the history of camel husbandry.

Epstein, Eliahu 1937. Transjordan: the nomad problem in Transjordan. *Palestine and Middle East Economic Magazine,* 9: 87–90. Tel Aviv.

Epstein, Eliahu 1938. Beduins of Transjordan: their social and economic problems. *Journ. R.C.A.S.* 25: 228–36. On the Bani Ṣakhr bedouin.

Epstein, Eliahu 1939. The economic situation of the Transjordan tribes. *Journ. R.C.A.S.* 26: 177–84.

Epstein, Eliahu 1939. Bedouin of the Negeb. *P.E.F.Q.*: 58–73.

Epstein, Eliahu 1948. Bedouin of the Negev. *Jewish Frontier,* 15: 30–34.

Euting, J. 1896. *Tagebuch einer Reise in Inner-Arabien.* 2 vols. Leiden: Brill. ('Journal of a journey in inner Arabia.')

Evans-Prichard, E. E. 1946. Topographical terms in common use among the bedouins of Cyrenaica. *J.R.A.I.* 76: 177–88.

Evans-Prichard, E. E. 1946. Italy and the bedouin in Cyrenaica. *African Affairs,* 45: 12–21.

Evans-Prichard, E. E. 1949. *The Sanusi of Cyrenaica.* Oxford: Clarendon Press. On the development of the Sanusi religious order among bedouin.

Feilberg, C. G. 1944. *La tente noire : contribution ethnographique à l'histoire des nomades.* Copenhagen: Nationalmuseeta Skrifter. Ethnografisk. Roekke II. Discusses the construction and distribution of the tent in Arabia, Asia and north Africa.

Fernea, Robert A. 1960. Cultural similarities and sociological differences between the nomadic and settled Arabs of Iraq. In *Actes du VI Congrès International des Sciences Anthropologiques et Ethnologiques.* 2: 71–75. Paris.

Fernea, Robert A. 1970. *Shaykh and Effendi : changing patterns of authority among the el-Shabana of southern Iraq.* Cambridge, Mass: Harvard Univ. Press. On settled agriculturalists descended from bedouin.

Field, Henry 1935. *Arabs of central Iraq, their history, ethnology and physical characters.* Chicago Natural History Museum: Anthropological Memoirs, 4.

Field, Henry 1952. *Anthropogeographical bibliography of the Persian Gulf area.* Mimeograph. Washington.

Field, Henry 1952. Camel brands and graffiti from Iraq, Syria, Jordan, Iran and Arabia. *Journ. of the American Oriental Society.* New Haven, Conn. Supplement 15.

Field, Henry and Glubb, J. B. 1943. *The Yezidis, Sulubba and other tribes of Iraq and adjacent regions* (bibliog.). Menasha: General Series in Anthropology, 10.

Fisher, W. B. 1958. *The Middle East: a physical, social and regional geography.* 2nd ed. London: Methuen. Standard reference work on the area.

* **Freer, A. M. Goodrich (H. H. Spoer)** 1924. *Arabs in Tent and Town: An intimate account of the family life of the Arabs of Syria with a description of the animals and plants of their country.* London: Seeley, Service and Co. (photos).

Gabrieli, Francesco 1959. *L'antica società beduina, studi di W. Dostal, G. Dossin, M. Höfner, J. Henninger, F. Gabrieli.* Roma: Università di Roma: Centro Studi Semitici 2. A collection of studies on the bedouin, see Dostal (1959) and Henninger (1959).

* **de Gaury, G.** 1950. *Arabian journey and other desert travels.* London: G. Harrap and Co.

Gennep, A. van 1902. Les *wasm,* ou marques de propriété des Arabes. *International Archiv für Ethnographie,* 15: 85–98. Leiden.

Glubb, J. B. 1937. Arab chivalry. *Journ. R.C.A.S.* 24: 5–26.

Glubb, J. B. 1938. The economic situation of the TransJordan tribes. *Journ. R.C.A.S.* 25: 449–459.

Glubb, J. B. 1942. The bedouins of northern Arabia. See: Crown, 1942.

Glubb, J. B. 1943. The Sulubba and other ignoble tribes of south western Asia. See Field, H. &. J. B. Glubb (1943).

Goodison, R. A. C. 1958. Arab dialect studies: Arabian Peninsula. *Middle East Journal,* 12 (2): 205–213. Washington.

Gräf, E. 1952. *Das Rechtswesen der heutigen Beduinen.* Walldorf-Hessen: Verlag für Orientkunde. On tribal law among north Arabian tribes.

Grant, C. P. 1937. *The Syrian desert: caravans, travel and exploration.* London: A. & C. Black (maps, glossary).

Great Britain: Admiralty, Naval Intelligence Division 1920. *A Handbook of Arabia. 1. General.* 2 vols. London: H.M.S.O. I.D. 1128. C.B. 405.

Great Britain: Admiralty, Naval Intelligence Division 1920. *A Handbook of Syria (including Palestine).* London: H.M.S.O. I.D. 1215.

Great Britain: Admiralty, Naval Intelligence Division 1943. *Syria.* Geographical Handbook Series.

Great Britain: Admiralty, Naval Intelligence Division 1943. *Palestine and TransJordan B.R. 514.* Geographical Handbook Series (bibliog.).

Great Britain: Admiralty, Naval Intelligence Division 1944. *Iraq and the Persian Gulf B.R. 524.* Sept. 1944. Geographical Handbook Series (illus., maps).

Great Britain: Admiralty, Naval Intelligence Division 1946. *Western Arabia and the Red Sea B.R. 527.* Oxford: Geographical Handbook Series.

Guamani, Carlo C. C. 1938. *Northern Negd. A journey from Jerusalem: Anaiza in Qusam.* London: Argonaut Press. Includes descriptions of the Shammar and the Wahhābī movement. Translated from Italian, Jerusalem: 1866.

Hardy, M. J. L. 1963. *Blood feuds and the payment of blood money in the Middle East.* Leiden: Brill.

Harik, Iliya 1972. The impact of the domestic market on rural-urban relations in the Middle East. In *Rural politics and social change in the Middle East*, ed. R. Antoun and Iliya Harik. London: Indiana Univ. Press: 337–363.

Harris, George L. et al. 1958. *Jordan: its people, its society, its culture.* New York: Grove Press.

Harris, George L. et al. 1958. *Iraq: its people, its society, its culture.* New Haven: *H.R.A.F.* (bibliog.).

Harrison, Paul W. 1924. *The Arab at home.* New York: T. Y. Crowell. On eastern Arabia, Muscat and the Arabian Gulf.

Hart, David M. 1962. The social structure of the Rgibat Bedouins of the western Sahara. *Middle East Journal*, 16 (4): 512–27. Washington.

Hartmann, R. 1938. Zur heutigen Lage des Beduinetums. In *Die Welt des Islam*, 20 (1938): 51–73. On changes in bedouin life due to Western influence.

Heard-Bey, Frauke 1974. Development anomalies in the bedouin oasis of al-Lima. *Asian Affairs. Journ. R.C.A.S.* 61 (n.s. vol. 5 part 3) Oct. On recently settled bedouin in Abu Dhabi.

Helaissi, A. S. 1959. The bedouins and tribal life in Saudi Arabia. *International Social Science Journal*, 11 (4): 532–38. Paris.

Henninger, J. 1939. Zur verbreitung des Brautpreises bei den arabischen Beduinen. *Anthropos*, 34: 380–88. Salzburg. ('Concerning the diffusion of brideprice among the Arabian bedouin.')

Henninger, J. 1943. Die Familie bei den heutigen Beduinen Arabiens und seiner Randgebiete. Ein Beitrag zur Frage der ursprunglichen Familienform der Semiten. *Int. Arch. für Eth.*, 42. ('On the modern Bedouin family and the problem of the origins of the Semitic family types.)

Henninger, J. 1950. Tribus et classes de parias en Arabie et en Egypte. *Actes du XIVe Congrès International de Sociologie* 4: 1–13. Rome.

Henninger, J. 1959. La société bedouine ancienne. In *l'antica società beduina*, ed. Francesco Gabrieli: 29–93. On pre-Islamic bedouin society.

Hess, Jean Jacques 1922. *Beduinennamen aus zentral Arabien*, vorgelegt von C. Bezold; Sitzungsberichte der Heidelberger Akademie der Wissenschaften. Jahresgang 1912. 19 Abbandlung. ('Bedouin names in central Arabia.')

Hess, Jean Jacques 1938. *Von den Beduinen des innern Arabiens: Erzählungen, Lieder, Sitten und Gebräuche.* Zurich and Leipzig: Niehans.

* **Hill, Gray** 1901. *With the bedouins: a narrative of journeys and adventures in unfrequented parts of Syria.* London: T. Fisher Unwin (First published 1891) (photos).

Hillelson, S. 1937–38. Notes on the bedouin tribes of Beersheba district. *P.E.F.Q.* 1937: 242–252 and 1938: 55–63. Notes taken from al-'Ārif (1935), with lists of tribes and information on law.

* **Ingrams, W. H.** 1942. *Arabia and the Isles.* London: John Murray. On south Arabian tribes and their pacification by the British.

Irons, W. 1965. Livestock raiding among pastoralists: an adaptive interpretation. In *Papers of the Michigan Academy of Science, Arts and Letters*, 50: 393–414.

Jacob, Dr. Georg 1895. *Das Leben der vorislamischen Beduinen.* Leipzig. ('Way of life of the pre-Islamic bedouin.')

Jacob, Dr. Georg 1897. *Altarabisches Beduinenleben nach den Quellen geschildert.* Berlin: Mayer & Müller (early photos).

al-Jamil, Makki 1956. *Al-badū wa'l-qabā'il al-rahhālah fi'l-'Irāq.* (Arabic). Baghdad. ('Bedouin and wandering tribes of Iraq.')

* **Jarvis, Claude S.** 1931. *Yesterday and today in Sinai.* Edinburgh and London.

Jarvis, Claude S. 1935. Sinai. *Journ. R.C.A.S.*, 22 (1): 32–51.

Jarvis, Claude S. 1936. The desert bedouin and his future. *Journ. R.C.A.S.*, 23: 585–93.

* **Jarvis, Claude S.** 1936. *Three deserts.* London: John Murray. On Sinai and the Western Desert.

Jarvis, Claude S. 1937. The desert yesterday and today. *P.E.F.Q.*: 116–25.

Jauhari, Rif'at. 1947. *Asrār min al-ṣaḥrā al-gharbīyah.* Cairo: Dar al-Ma'ārif. On the Western Desert of Egypt.

* **Jaussen, P. Antonin** 1908. *Coûtumes des arabes au pays de Moab.* Paris. Reprinted 1948. Paris: Adrien-Maisonneuve.

Jennings-Bramley, W. S. 1900. Sport among the bedawin. *P.E.F.Q.*: 369–76. On hunting.

* **Jennings-Bramley, W. S.** 1905–14. The bedouin of the Sinaitic Peninsula. *P.E.F.Q.*: 1905: 126–136, 211; 1906: 23–33, 103–109, 197–205, 250–8; 1907: 22–33, 131–137, 279–284; 1908: 30–36, 112–116; 1909: 253–258; 1910: 140; 1911: 34–42, 172–181: 1912: 13–20, 62–68; 1913: 34–38, 79–84; 1914: 9–17, 24, 129–133. On all aspects of bedouin life.

Jessup, H. H. 1910. *Fifty-three years in Syria.* 2 vols. New York: Fleming H. Revell Co.

Johnson, Douglas L. 1973. *Jabal al-Akhdar, Cyrenaica: an historical geography of settlement and livelihood.* Univ. of Chicago, Dept. of Geography Research Paper no. 148.

Johnson, F. 1918. Some bedouin customs. *Man*, 18: 6–8, London.

Johnstone, T. M. 1961. Some characteristics of the Dosiri dialect of Arabic as spoken in Kuwait. *Bull. S.O.A.S.* 24: 249–97. Concerning a conversation on camel husbandry.

Johnstone, T. M. and Wilkinson, J. C. 1960. Some geographical aspects of Qatar. *Geographical Journal*, 126: 442–50. London.

Kahle, P. 1913. Die Aulād 'Ali-Beduinen der Libyschen wüste. In *Der Islam*. Strasburg, 4: 355–386. ('The 'Awlād 'Āli bedouin of the Libyan desert.')

Kaselau, A. 1927. *Die freuen Beduinen nord und zentral Arabiens*. Hamburg: Universitat.

Kelly, John B. 1964. *Eastern arabian frontiers*. London: Faber & Faber (tribal lists, maps, bibliog.). On disputed claims to the Buraimi oasis.

Kelly, John B. 1972. A prevalence of furies: tribes, politics and religion in Oman and Trucial Oman. In *The Arabian Peninsula: society and politics*, ed. D. Hopwood. London: Allen and Unwin.

Kennet, A. 1925. *Beduin justice: laws and customs among the Egyptian beduin*. Cambridge.

Kiḥālah, 'Amr 1949. *Mu'jam Qabā'il al-'Arab al-Qadīmah wa'l-Ḥadīthah*. (Arabic). An encyclopaedia of ancient and modern bedouin tribes in the Middle East.

Lancaster, F. 1974. Bedouin by adoption. *New Society*. 591: 245–6. London. By an anthropologist living with her family among the Rwāla bedouin.

Landberg, Count Carlo von 1897. *Arabica no: IV, Notes préliminaires sur les tribus du pays libre de Datīna et du Sultanat des 'Awāliq supérieurs*. etc. 2 vols. Leide.

Landberg, Count Carlo von 1970. *Chez les bédouins: récit arabes. Publié d'après un manuscript de la Bibliothèque de L'Université d'Uppsala par A. Albert Kudzi-Zadeh*. Leiden: Brill.

* **Lawrence, T. E.** 1935. *Seven pillars of wisdom*. London: Jonathan Cape. On the Arab Revolt in the Great War with descriptions of bedouin personalities and customs.

* **Lees, Rev G. Robinson** 1909. *The witness of the wilderness. The bedawin of the desert. Their origin, history, home life, strife, religion and superstitions, in their relation to the Bible*. London: Longman.

Lewando-Hundt, Gillian. 1973. A progress report on fieldwork amongst bedouin women. In *Notes on the Bedouin*: Midrashat Sde-Boker Field School, Israel.

Lewis, N. 1955. The frontier of settlement in Syria 1800–1950. *International Affairs*, 31 (Jan.): 48–60.

Lienhardt, P. A. 1953–4. *The northern arabs: an account of the social and political organisation of some nomad and settled communities of northern Arabia and greater Syria*. Oxford Univ. thesis.

Lipsky, George A. et al. 1959. *Saudi Arabia: its people, its society, its culture*. New Haven, *H.R.A.F.* (bibliog.).

* **Lorimer, J. G.** 1908–15. *Gazetteer of the Persian Gulf, 'Oman and central Arabia*. 2 vols. in four parts. India: Government. Historical, geographical and economic survey including location of tribes.

Macdonald, A. D. 1936. The political development in Iraq: 1935. *Journ. R.C.A.S.*

Macro, Eric 1958. *Bibliography of the Arabian peninsula.* Univ. of Miami Press.

Mahhouk, Adnan 1956. Recent agricultural development and bedouin settlement in Syria. *Middle East Journal,* 10: 167–76. Washington.

Maoz, Moshe 1960. *Ottoman reform in Syria and Palestine, 1840–1861. The impact of the Tanzimat on politics and society.* Oxford: Clarendon Press.

* **Marx, Emanuel** 1967. *Bedouin of the Negev.* Manchester: Manchester University Press.

Marx, Emanuel 1973a. Circumcision feasts among Negev bedouin. *International Journal of Middle Eastern Studies,* 4: 411–427. Cambridge.

Marx, Emanuel 1973b. The organisation of nomadic groups in the Middle East. In *Society and Political Structure in the Arab World,* ed. M. Milson. New York: Humanities Press.

Matthews, C. D. 1960. Bedouin life in contemporary Arabia. *Rivista degli Studi Orientali,* 35 (1–2): 31–61.

Mayeux, F. J. 1816. *Les Bédouins.* 3 vols. Paris.

Meulen, van der D. 1947. *Aden to the Hadramaut, a journey in south Arabia.* London.

Miles, S. B. 1881. Notes on the tribes of Oman. In *Selections from the records no. 181 : administration report of the Persian Gulf,* 1880–81 : 29–44.

* **Miles, S. B.** 1966. *The countries and tribes of the Persian Gulf.* With a new introduction by J. B. Kelly. 2 vols. in one (2nd ed.). London: Cass. First published 1919.

Milne, J. C. M. 1971. *The problem of patrilateral parallel cousin marriage with special reference to a southern Jordan village, el-Jai,* University of Edinburgh, M.A. thesis. On recently settled Ḥuwayṭāt.

Mohsen, Safia K. 1967. The legal status of women among the Awlad Ali. *Anthropological Quarterly,* 40: 153–166. Washington. On the bedouin in the Western Desert of Egypt.

Montagne, R. 1932. Notes sur la vie sociale et politique de l'Arabie du Nord: les Šammar du Negd. *Revue des Études Islamiques,* 6 :61–79. Paris.

Montagne, R. 1935. Contes poétiques bédouins (recueillis chez les Šammar de Gezīré). *Bull. d'Études Orientales* 6: 33–120. Paris: L'Institut Français de Damas.

Montagne, R. 1947. *La civilization du désert : nomades d'Orient et d'Afrique.* Paris: Le Tour du Monde. On Saudi tribes especially Shammar.

Muhsam, H. V. 1951. Some notes on bedu marriage habits. In *Proceedings of the fourteenth International Congress of Sociology,* 4: 297–316. Reprinted in Muhsam (1966). Gives statistics.

Muhsam, H. V. 1953. Aspects of the structure of the family of villagers and bedouins in Palestine. In *Proceedings of the sixteenth International Congress of Sociology*. Reprinted in Muhsam 1966. Based on 1946 census of households.

Muhsam, H. V. 1959. Sedentarisation of the beduin in Israel. In *International Social Science Journal (2) Nomads and nomadism in the arid zone*: 539–549. Reprinted in Muhsam 1966.

Muhsam, H. V. 1966. *Beduin of the Negev – Eight Demographic Studies*. Jerusalem: The Eliezer Kaplan School of Economics and Social Sciences, Hebrew University.

Müller, Victor 1931. *En Syrie avec les bédouins*. Paris: Librairie Ernest Leroux. On territories and social and political organisation.

Murphy, R. F. and Kasdan, I. 1959. The structure of parallel cousin marriage. *American Anthropologist*, 61: 17–29. New York. On the Levant area.

* **Murray, G. W.** 1935. *Sons of Ishmael: A study of the Egyptian beduin*. London: George Routledge & Sons (illus.). Reprinted 1967. Based on 25 years' surveying experience.

* **Musil, Alois** 1908. *Arabia Petraea*. 3 vols. Vienna (in German). Vol. 3 on nomads of east Jordan (Transjordan).

Musil, Alois 1926. *The northern Hegaz-a topographical itinerary*. New York: American Geographical Society. On Shararat, 'Imrān, Ḥuwayṭāt, and Bani 'Aṭīyah bedouin, based on a journey in 1910.

Musil, Alois 1927. *Arabia Deserta: a topographical itinerary*. New York: American Geographical Society. On journeys 1908–15 in north Arabia, especially among Rwāla, 'Amarāt, Salubba, 'Awlad 'Āli and Shararāt.

Musil, Alois 1928a. *Northern Neǧd: a topographical itinerary*. New York: American Geographical Society. Based on journey in 1915 in the Nefud. On the Shammar, 'Awlad Slayman, Hutaym and al-Zafir bedouin, and on the histories of the Rashid and Sa'ūd leading families.

* **Musil, Alois** 1928b. *The manners and customs of the Rwala bedouins*. New York: American Geographical Society. 6. Information collected in 1908–9.

Musil, Alois 1928c. *Palmyrena: a topographical itinerary*. New York: American Geographical Society 14. From journeys of 1908, 1912 and 1915. On Rwala, 'Umur, Fwā're, Bani Khalid, Mwāli, Sba'a, and Ḥadidiyīn bedouin.

Musil, Alois and Glubb, J. B. 1948. The complicated lives of desert nomads: the Ruwalla beduin. In *A Reader in General Anthropology*, ed. Carleton S. Coon: 380–407. New York: Holt, Rinehart & Winston.

Nelson, C. 1973. *The desert and the sown: nomads in the wider society*. Berkeley: Institute of International Studies, University of California.

Nevins, E. and Wright, Theon 1969. *World without time: the bedouin*. New York: John Day Co. On a journey to find evidence of T. E. Lawrence's travels among the Jordanian bedouin.

Niebuhr, Carsten 1799. *Travels through Arabia and other countries in the east*. Perth, Reprinted: Librairie du Liban, Beirut.

Oppenheim, Max von 1949–68. *Die Beduinen*. Leipzig and Wiesbaden: Unter Mitbearbeitung von Erich Braunlich und Werner Caskel. 4 vols. (bibliog.). Comprehensive work on bedouin genealogies and territories.

Oxtoby, Willard G. 1968. *Some inscriptions of the Safaitic bedouin*. New Haven.

Palgrave, W. G. 1868. *Personal narrative of a year's journey through central and eastern Arabia*. London: Macmillan and Co.

Palmer, E. H. 1871. *The desert of the Exodus*. 2 vols. Cambridge: Deighton, Bell & Co.

Pasner, Stephen 1971. Camel, sheep and nomad social organisation: a comment on Rubel's model. *Man* (N.S. 6:2) 285–8. London. On the Rwāla bedouin.

Patai, R. 1951. Nomadism: Middle Eastern and Central Asian. *S.W.J.A.* 7: 401–14.

Patai, R. 1956. *The Hashemite Kingdom of Jordan*. Country Survey Series, 4. New Haven: *H.R.A.F.*

Patai, R. 1956. *The Republic of Syria*. 2 vols. New Haven: *H.R.A.F.*

Patai, R. 1958. *The Hashemite Kingdom of Jordan*. Princeton: Princeton University Press.

Peake, F. G. 1958. *A History of Jordan and its Tribes*. 2 vols. Florida: Coral Gables. Arabic version first published in Amman, 1934.

Parshits, A. I. 1966. The nomad economy in Saudi Arabia. In *The Economic History of the Middle East 1800–1914*, ed. C. Issawi. Chicago and London: University of Chicago Press.

Peters, Emrys L. 1951. *The sociology of the bedouin of Cyrenaica*. Oxford University: Lincoln College, PhD thesis.

Peters, Emrys L. 1960, The proliferation of segments in the lineage of the bedouin of Cyrenaica. *J.R.A.I.* 90 (1): 29–53. Reprinted in Sweet (1970).

Peters, Emrys L. 1963. The tied and the free: an account of a type of patron-client relationship among the bedouin pastoralists of Cyrenaica. In *Contributions to Mediterranean Sociology. Mediterranean Rural Communities and Social Change*, ed. J. G. Peristiany. 167–188. Paris and The Hague: Mouton & Co.

Peters, Emrys L. 1965. Aspects of the family among the bedouin of Cyrenaica. In *Comparative family systems*, ed. M. F. Nimkoff. 121–146. Boston.

Peters, Emrys L. 1967. Some structural aspects of the feud among the camel herding bedouin in Cyrenaica. *Africa*, 37 (3): 261–82. London.

Peters, Stella 1952. *A study of the bedouin (Cyrenaica) bait*. Oxford: St. Hilda's College. B.Litt thesis. On every aspect of the bedouin tent.

Philby, H. St. J. B. 1928. *Arabia of the Wahhabis*. London: Constable & Co.

Philby, H. St. J. B. 1933. *The Empty Quarter: being a description of the great south desert of Arabia known as Rub' al Khali.* New York: H. Holt & Co. Includes material on the Murrah bedouin.

Philby, H. St. J. B. 1952. *Arabian Highlands.* New York: Ithaca.

Randolph, R. R. 1963. *Elements in the social structure of the Qdiirat Beduin.* Houston: Rice University. Ph.D. thesis.

Raswan, Carl R. 1922. *Les tribus arabes de Syrie.* Beirut.

Raswan, Carl R. 1929a. From tent to tent among the bedouins who are faithful to the ancient Arabian code of boundless hospitality. *Asia,* 29, 570–76, 578–80.

Raswan, Carl R. 1929b. The eaglet of the Sha'alān in the Ruala tents. *Asia,* 29: 364–70, 427–31.

Raswan, Carl R. 1930. Tribal areas and migration lines of the north Arabian beduins. *Geographical Review,* 20: 494–502 (map).

Raswan, Carl R. 1936. *Moeurs et coûtumes des bédouins.* Paris. On the Rwāla bedouin.

Raswan, Carl R. 1945. Vocabulary of bedouin words concerning horses. *Journal of Near Eastern Studies,* 4 (2) Chicago: 97–129.

* **Raswan, Carl R.** 1947. *The black tents of Arabia (my life amongst the beduins).* New York: Creative Age Press. Glossary. Also published in German, 1934. On the Rwāla bedouin.

al-Rāwī, 'Abd al-Jabbār 1949. *Al-bādīyah.* Baghdad: al-'Amī Press. (Arabic). On the bedouin of Iraq.

Roberts, Arthur Henry 1928. Bedouin hospitality. *Asia,* 28: 878–81, 935–38.

Roberts, Arthur Henry 1928. Bedouin justice. *Asia,* 28: 600–5, 666–67.

Rosenfeld, H. 1951. *The military occupational specialization of the kin: a key to the process of caste formation in the Arabian desert.* Columbia Univ. Ph.D. dissertation.

Rosenfeld, H. 1965. The social composition of the military in the Arabian desert. *J.R.A.I.,* 95 (1): 75–86, 174–194. On the dynasty of the Ibn Rashīd at Hai'l in the northern Nejd from the 1830's to the early 1900's.

Rubel, Paula G. 1969. Herd composition and social structure: on building models of nomadic pastoral societies. *Man* (N.S.) 4: 2: 268–273. London. On differences between the Rwāla bedouin, Somalis, Cyrenaica bedouin and non-bedouin shepherd tribes.

Salīm, Shakir Musṭafā 1962. *Marsh Dwellers of the Euphrates Delta.* London: Athlone Press. L.S.E. Monographs on Social Anthropolgy, 23. On Iraqi Arabs of desert origin who have settled.

Seabrook, W. B. 1928. *Adventures in Arabia.* London. (illus.).

Serjeant, R. B. 1953. Notes on Ṣubaiḥi territory west of Aden. *Le Muséon,* 66: 123–31. On camel breeders and cultivators who possess a star calendar.

Sharon, Moshe 1976. The bedouins of the Hebron Hills. (Hebrew). In *Judea and Samaria*, ed. A. Shmueli. University of Tel Aviv.

Shkolnik, A. (et al) 1972. Water economy of the bedouin goat. In *Symposia of the Zoological Society of London*, 31.

Shmueli, Avshalom 1969/70. *Hitnahalut ha-beduyin shel midbar yehudah* (Hebrew). Tel Aviv: Goma, M.A. thesis Hebrew University, Jerusalem. ('Bedouin settlement in the Judean Hills.') On the settled Ta'āmreh bedouin, near Bethlehem.

Shmueli, Avshalom 1973. *The sedentarisation of nomads in the vicinity of Jerusalem in the twentieth century.* (Hebrew). Jerusalem: Hebrew University. Ph.D. thesis.

Shuqayr, Naum 1916. *Tā'rīkh sīnā al-qadīm wa'l-ḥadīth wa jirghāfīyatihā.* (Arabic). Cairo: Dār al-Ma'ārif ('History and geography of ancient and modern Sinai.')

Smith, W. Robertson 1885. *Kinship and marriage in early Arabia.* ed. S. A. Cook. London: Adam & Charles Black, reprinted by Beacon Press: Boston.

Smith, W. Robertson 1889. *Lectures on the religion of the Semites.* London: Black.

Sonnen, P. J. 1952. *Die Beduinen um See Genesareth . . . ihre Lebensbedingungen, soziale Struktur, Religion und Rechtsverhältnisse.* Mit einem Geleitwort von O. Spier-Bonn. Köln: Bachem. ('The Bedouin around the sea of Galilee . . . on their way of life, social structure, religion and legal procedures.')

Stein, Lothar 1967. *Die Šammar-Ǧerba. Beduinen im übergang von Nomadismus zur Sesshaftigkeit.* Berlin: Akademie Verlag. On the settlement of the nomadic Shammar tribes on agriculturally marginal land.

Sweet, Louise E. 1960. *Tell Toqaan : A Syrian village.* University of Michigan (illus.). On settled bedouin.

Sweet, Louise E. 1965a. Camel raiding of north Arabian bedouin : a mechanism of ecological adaptation. *American Anthropologist*, 67: 1132–50. New York. On the bedouin of Kuwait. Reprinted in Sweet (1970).

Sweet, Louise E. 1965b. Camel pastoralism in north Arabia and the minimal camping unit. In *Man, culture and animals : the role of animals in human ecological adjustments*, ed. A. Leeds and A. P. Vayda. Washington, D.C.: American Association of the Advancement of Science: 129–52. On Kuwait bedouin.

⋆ **Sweet, Louise E.** ed. 1970. *Peoples and cultures of the Middle East : an anthropological reader. Vol. 1. Depth and Diversity.* New York: Natural History Press. Collection of articles including Doughty (1936), Sweet (1965a) and Peters (1960).

⋆ **Sweet, Louise E.** 1971. *The Central Middle East : A handbook of anthropology and published research on the Nile Valley, the Arab Levant, southern Mesopotamia, the Arabian peninsula and Israel.* New Haven: *H.R.A.F.* Especially relevant: L. E. Sweet, The Arabian Peninsula: 271–355.

Tannous, 'Afif, I. 1947. The Arab tribal community in a nationalist state. *Middle East Journal*, I: 5–17. Washington.

Thesiger, W. 1948–9. Wolves of the desert: the Sa'ar tribe at the watering place. *Geographical Magazine*, 21: 394–400. London.

Thesiger, W. 1950. The badu of southern Arabia. *Journ. R.C.A.S.*, 37: 53–61.

* **Thesiger, W.** 1959. *Arabian Sands.* London: Longman. Record of journeys in 1945–50. Includes information on the pastoral tribes of the Rub' al-Khāli (Empty Quarter) area.

* **Thesiger, W.** 1964. *The Marsh Arabs.* London: Longman. On the tribes of the marshes at the junction of the Tigris and Euphrates.

Thomas, B. S. 1929. Among some unknown tribes of south Arabia. *J.R.A.I.*, 59: 97–111 (illus.). On the Hadara group of the Dhufar region.

Thomas, B. S. 1932. *Arabia Felix: across the Empty Quarter of Arabia.* London: Jonathan Cape.

Thoumin, Richard 1933. De la vie nomade à la vie sédentaire: un village Syrien: Adra. In *Mélanges Géographiques offerts par ses éléves à Raoul Blanchard.* Grenoble: 621–41.

Trial, George T. and **Winder, R. Bayley** 1922. *Les tribus arabes de Syrie.* Beirut.

Tristram, H. M. 1873. *The land of Moab. Travels and discoveries on the east side of the Dead Sea and the Jordan.* London: John Murray.

Tweedie, W. 1961. *The Arabian horse: his country and people.* Los Angeles. First published, 1894.

Upton, R. D. 1877. On the bedaween of the Arabian Desert. In *Frazer's Magazine* (N.S.) 15: 432–443. London.

Upton, R. D. 1881. *Gleanings from the desert of Arabia.* London.

Vinogradov, A. 1972. The 1920 revolt in Iraq reconsidered: the role of the tribes in national politics, *Middle Eastern Studies.*

Weir, Shelagh 1970. *Spinning and Weaving in Palestine.* London: British Museum.

Weir, Shelagh 1973. A bridal headdress from southern Palestine. *P.E.Q.*, 105: 101–9.

Weir, Shelagh 1975. Some observations on pottery and weaving in the Yemen Arab Republic. In *Proceedings of the Seminar for Arabian Studies*, 5: 65–76. London.

Zeller, Rev. John 1901. The bedawin. *P.E.F.Q.*: 185–202.